EVERY DAY COUNTS®

PRACTICE COUNTS

Patsy F. Kanter • Janet G. Gillespie • Andy Clark

GRADE
1

GReaT SouRCe®
EDUCATION GROUP
A Houghton Mifflin Company
New Ways to Know™

Printed in the United States of America

Great Source® and Every Day Counts® are registered trademarks of Houghton Mifflin Company.

International Standard Book Number -13: 978-0–669–46940–0

International Standard Book Number -10: 0–669–46940–8

8 9 10 CRK 07 06

URL address: http://www.greatsource.com/

Write how many.

1.

2.

3.

4.

_____
— — — — — —
_____

5.

6.

7.

8.

_____
— — — — — —
_____

Color the △ red 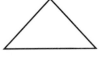.

Color the ▭ blue .

9.   A   B   A   B   A   B

Write how many tags.

1.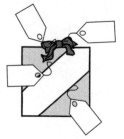

2.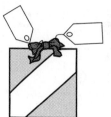

3.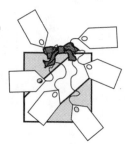

4.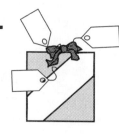

_____
- - - - - -
_____

5.

6.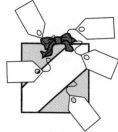

7.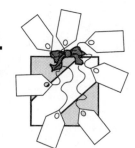

8.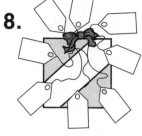

_____
- - - - - -
_____

Look at the box. Write the answer.

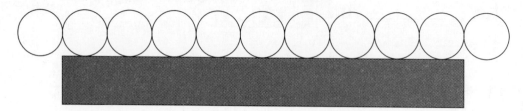

_____
- - - - - -

9. How many circles fit in the box?

_____

DAY 3

Write how many.

1.

2.

3.

4.

_____
- - - - - - - -
_____

5.

6.

7.

8.

_____
- - - - - - - -
_____

Color the shapes with 4 sides blue .

9.

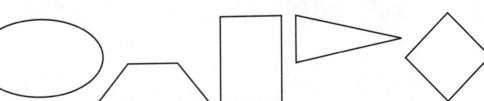

DAY 4

Write how many.

1.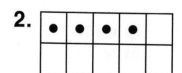

_____

- - - - - - -

_____

2.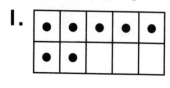

_____

- - - - - - -

_____

3.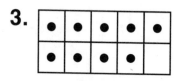

_____

- - - - - - -

_____

4.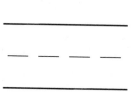

_____

- - - - - - -

_____

5.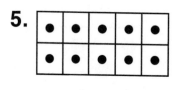

_____

- - - - - - -

_____

6.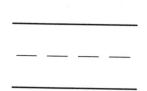

_____

- - - - - - -

_____

Solve.

7. I see cats and dogs. How many cats do you see?

_____

- - - - - - -

_____ cats

DAY 5

Circle a set of 5 suns.

1.

_____

_ _ _ _ _

2. How many suns all together? _____

Draw a picture to show more umbrellas than suns.

3.

DAY 6

Write how many.

1. _____

2. _____

3. _____

4.  _____

5. _____

6. _____

7. _____

8.  _____

Make 10 marks.

9.

Color the ⬭ green green .

Color the ○ blue blue .

10.

A   A   B   A   A   B   A   A   B

DAY 7

Draw dots.

1.

2.

3.

4.

5.

6.

7.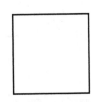

8.

9. How many dots did you draw above? _____

Write how many minutes.

10.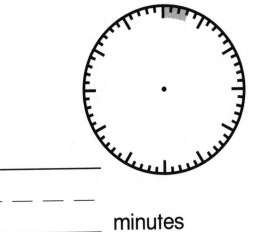

_____

_ _ _ _

_____ minutes

11.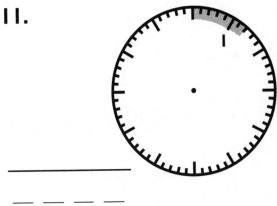

_____

_ _ _ _

_____ minutes

Write the missing numbers.

1.

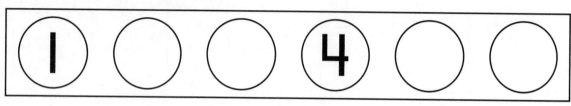

2.

Write how many sides.

3.
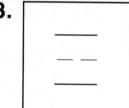

4.
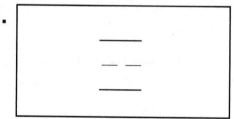

5.
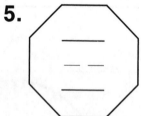

6.
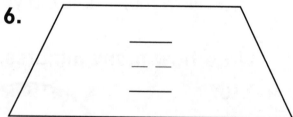

7.

8.
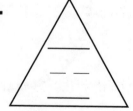

DAY 9

Circle sets of 5.

1.

_____

_ _ _ _ _

2. How many sets? _____

Answer each question.

Sunday	Monday	Tuesday	Wednesday	Thursday	Friday	Saturday

_____

_ _ _ _ _ _ _

3. What day comes before Tuesday? _____

_____

_ _ _ _ _ _ _

4. What day comes after Thursday? _____

_____

_ _ _ _

5. How many days are in a week? _____

_____

_ _ _ _

6. How many days a week do you
   come to school? _____

DAY 10 CHECKPOINT

Match.

1.   9   4   8   2   5

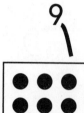

Use a green 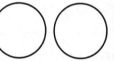 **and a yellow**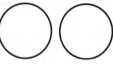
to make a pattern.

2.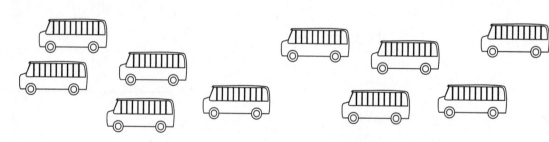

Circle sets of 5.

_____

_ _ _ _ _

3. How many sets of 5?   _____

Draw a shape with 3 sides.

4.

DAY 11

Count the dots. Write the number that comes next.

1. 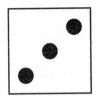 _ _ _ _ _

2. _ _ _ _ _

3. _ _ _ _ _

4. _ _ _ _ _

5. _ _ _ _ _

6. _ _ _ _ _

Color the red .

Color the purple .

7.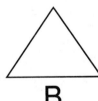

   A   B   B   A   B   B

Continue the pattern from above.

8.

_____   _____   _____   _____

DAY 12

Write what comes before.

1. _____ 3

2. _____ 10

3. _____ 1

4. _____ 7

5. _____ 5

6. _____ 8

Write how many minutes.

7.

☐ ☐ : ☐ ☐

8.
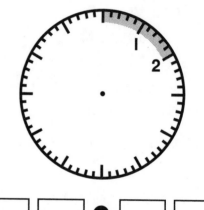

☐ ☐ : ☐ ☐

9.
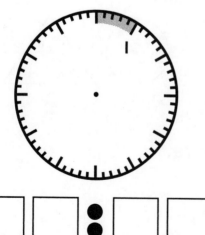

☐ ☐ : ☐ ☐

10.
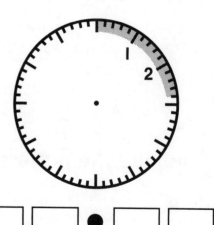

☐ ☐ : ☐ ☐

DAY 13

Write the missing numbers.

1.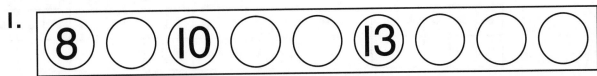
⑧ ◯ ⑩ ◯ ◯ ⑬ ◯ ◯ ◯

2.
⑤ ◯ ◯ ⑧ ◯ ◯ ⑪ ◯ ◯

Look at the picture. _____

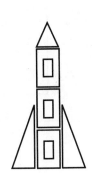

3. How many ▭ ? _____

4. How many 3-sided shapes?

_____

_____

Draw a picture. Use 3 ◯.

5.

DAY 14

Write how many.

1.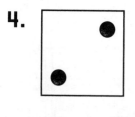

   _____

   _ _ _ _ _ _ _ _

   _____

2.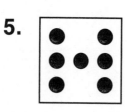

   _____

   _ _ _ _ _ _ _ _

   _____

3.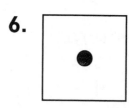

   _____

   _ _ _ _ _ _ _ _

   _____

4.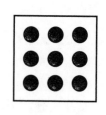

   _____

   _ _ _ _ _ _ _ _

   _____

5.

   _____

   _ _ _ _ _ _ _ _

   _____

6.

   _____

   _ _ _ _ _ _ _ _

   _____

7.

   _____

   _ _ _ _ _ _ _ _

   _____

Look at the Calendar.

8. How many children have a birthday in September?

   _____

   _ _ _ _ _ _ _ _

   _____ children

9. How many birthdays are in your class?

   _____

   _ _ _ _ _ _ _ _

   _____

DAY 15

Write the numbers in order.

1. 8, 9, 7   _____ _____ _____

2. 3, 1, 2   _____ _____ _____

3. 5, 4, 6   _____ _____ _____

4. 9, 8, 10   _____ _____ _____

Make a pattern.

5. 6 apples are on the table.
   3 are green and 3 are yellow.

DAY 16

Write how many.

1.

2.

3.

4.

_____

_ _ _ _ _ _ _ _

_____

5.

6.

7.

8.

_____

_ _ _ _ _ _ _ _

_____

Color the ◯ blue .

Color the ▭ red .

9. ◯   ▭   ◯   ▭   ◯   ▭

A   B   A   B   A   B

◯   ▭   ◯   ▭   ◯   ▭

A   B   A   B   A   B

DAY 17

Circle sets of 5.

I.

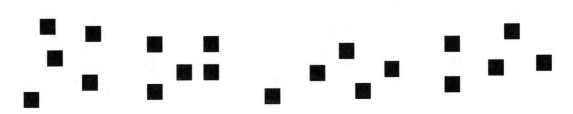

_____
_ _ _ _

2. How many sets of 5? _____

Look at the box. Write the answer.

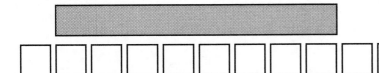

_____
_ _ _ _

3. How many squares fit in the box? _____

Look at the shapes.

Color the longest shape green 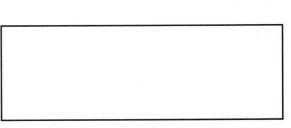.

4.

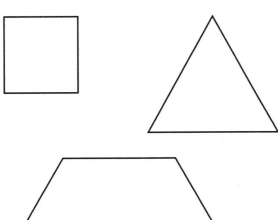

DAY 18

Write the missing numbers.

1.

2.

Trace and draw.

3. 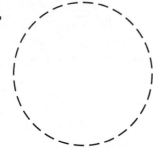 circle

4. square

5. 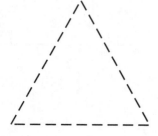 triangle

DAY 19

Write what comes after.

1. 1 _____

2. 2 _____

3. 3 _____

4. 4 _____

5. 5 _____

6. 6 _____

7. 7 _____

8. 8 _____

9. 9 _____

Look at the picture. Write how many.

10. _____ big rocks

11. _____ small rocks

12. There are _____ rocks all together.

DAY 20

Match.

1. 4   5

2. 6   7

3. 1   2   3

Draw a picture.

Use 4 [   ] .

4.

MONTHLY ASSESSMENT

Use a green 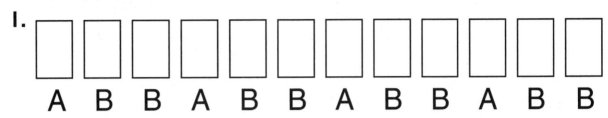 and a yellow .
Color the pattern.

1.

A	B	B	A	B	B	A	B	B	A	B	B

Color the same pattern on the Calendar.

2.

_____

— — — — —

3. What number comes before 7? _____

MONTHLY ASSESSMENT

Write how many.

1. _____

2. _____

Write the missing numbers.

3.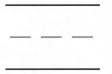

Write the number that comes before.

4. _____

5. _____

Match.

6.   5   6   7   8

        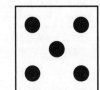

MONTHLY ASSESSMENT

Write how many minutes.

1.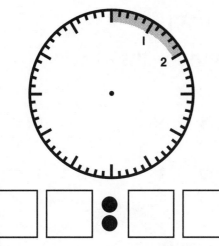

□ □ : □ □

2.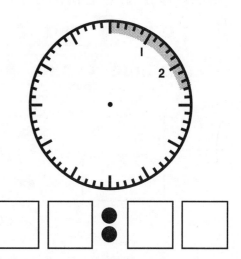

□ □ : □ □

Color the shapes with 4 sides red .

Color the shapes with 3 sides green .

3.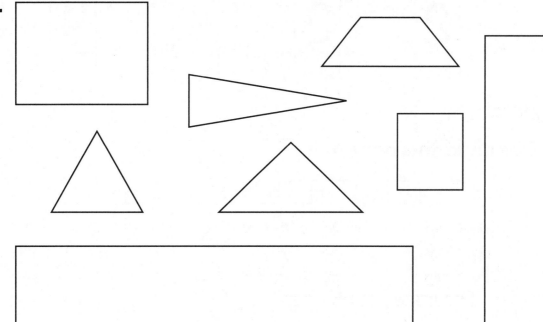

DAY 1 •••••••••••••••••••••••••••••••• OCTOBER

The 1's are connected.

Use a red 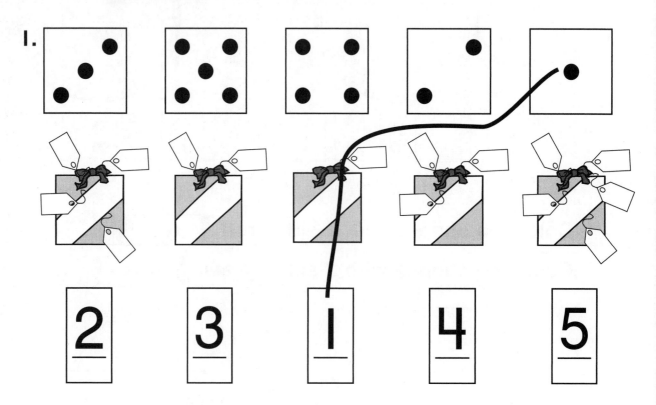 red ▷ to connect the 3's.

Use a blue | blue ▷ to connect the 4's.

1.

Continue the pattern.

2. ☐ ☐ ☐ ○ ☐ ☐ ☐ ○ ☐ ☐ ☐ ○ ☐

_____ _____ _____ _____

3. Draw the next 5 shapes.

_____ _____ _____ _____ _____

DAY 2

Use a red [red] to connect the 5's.

Use a blue [blue] to connect the 2's.

1.

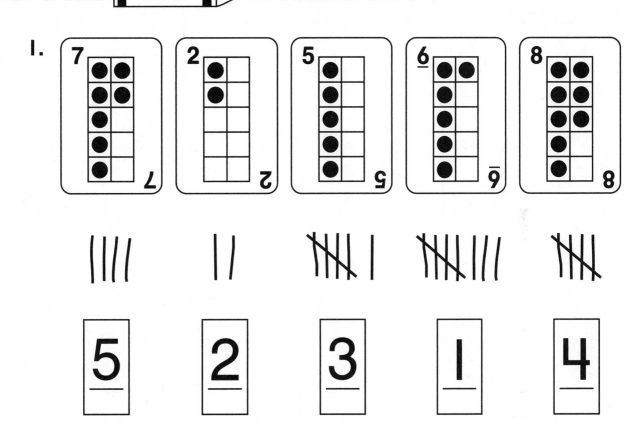

Which is longer? Draw an X on it.

2.

Day 3

Connect pictures of 6.

Connect pictures of 3.

1.

Draw a ring around the triangle.

2.

  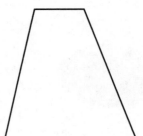 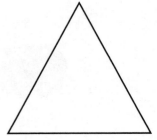

DAY 4

Connect pictures of 7.

Connect pictures of 5.

I.

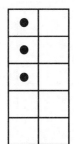 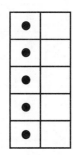 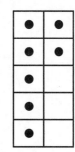 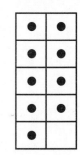

| 9 | 7 | 5 | 3 |

Look at the tags.

2. How many tags are there all together? Draw them.

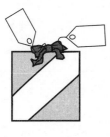 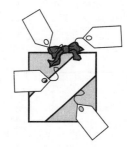

_____   _____   _____

_ _ _   **+**   _ _ _   **=**   _ _ _

_____   _____   _____

DAY 5

Connect pictures of 8.

Connect pictures of 3.

1.

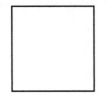

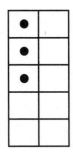 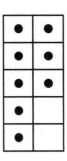  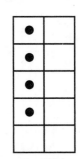 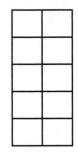

 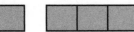  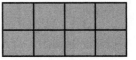

Draw something that has the same number.

2.

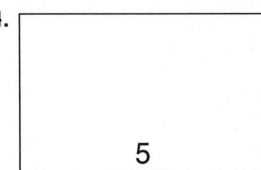

12

3.

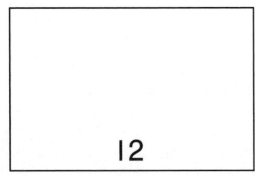

2

4.

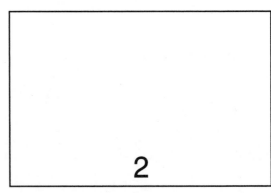

5

5.

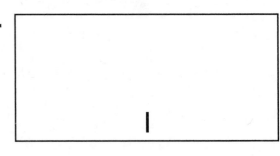

1

DAY 6

Connect pictures of 10.

Connect pictures of 5.

1.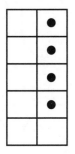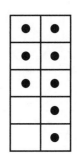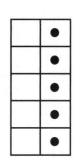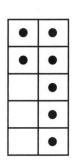

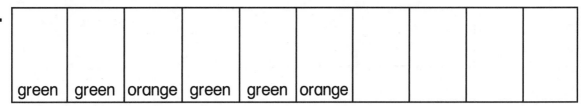

Color the pattern.

Use green | green ▷ and orange | orange ▷.

2.

green	green	orange	green	green	orange				

Complete the pattern.

3. A A B A A B ___ ___ ___

DAY 7

Write the missing numbers.

1.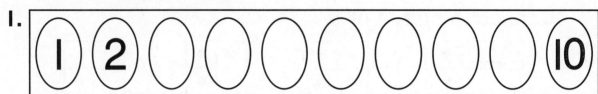

2.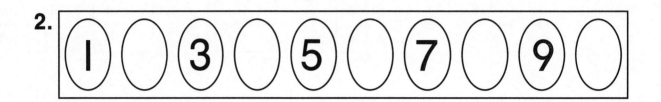

3.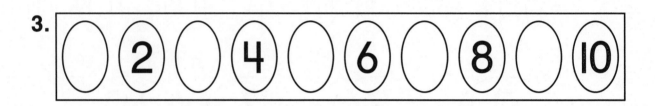

Color the larger shape blue | blue |▷.

Color the smaller shape green | green |▷.

4.

DAY 8

Draw I more dot. Write the number.

1.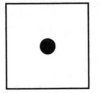

    1   _____

2.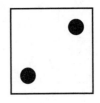

    2   _____

3.

    3   _____

4.

    4   _____

Circle sets of 10.

5.

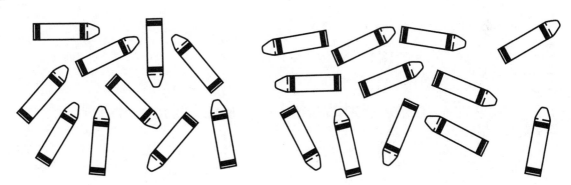

6. How many sets of 10? _____

7. How many extras? _____

DAY 9

Draw 1 less dot. Write the number.

1.   4 _____

2. 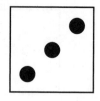 3 _____

3.   2 _____

4.   1 _____

Look at the pumpkins.

5. How many pumpkins are there all together?

_____ + _____ = _____

6. Make 5 another way.

_____ + _____ = _____

Add 1 more.

1. 4 _____ 2. 8 _____ 3. 0 _____

Draw one less dot.

4.   5.

Continue the pattern.

6. _____ _____ _____ _____ _____

Draw a big triangle.

7.

8. Draw a set of 10 marbles inside the triangle.

Add.

9. _____ + _____ = _____

DAY 11

Write how many dots.

1. 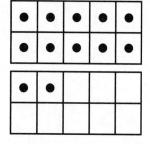 _____

2. 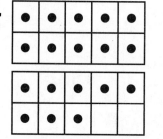 _____

3. 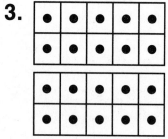 _____

4. 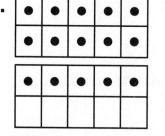 _____

5. 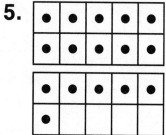 _____

6. 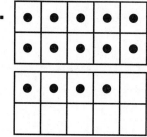 _____

Continue the patterns.

7.

8. 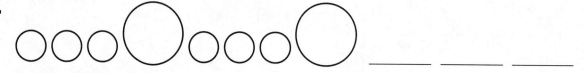 ___ ___ ___

Label the circle pattern.

9. ___ ___ ___ ___ ___ ___ ___ ___

DAY 12

Make 5.

1.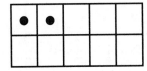

$$2 + \underline{\hspace{1.5cm}} = 5$$

2.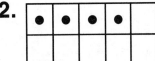

$$4 + \underline{\hspace{1.5cm}} = 5$$

3.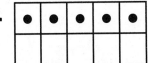

$$5 + \underline{\hspace{1.5cm}} = 5$$

4.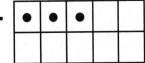

$$3 + \underline{\hspace{1.5cm}} = 5$$

5.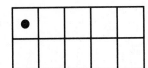

$$1 + \underline{\hspace{1.5cm}} = 5$$

6.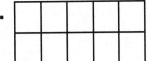

$$0 + \underline{\hspace{1.5cm}} = 5$$

Write how many minutes.

7.

$$\underline{\hspace{2cm}} \text{ minutes}$$

8.

$$\underline{\hspace{2cm}} \text{ minutes}$$

Write the missing numbers.

1.

1	2			5
6		8		
		13		15
	17		19	
21				25
	27	28		

Draw a picture inside the rectangle.

Use 3 triangles

△ △ △

2.

2 squares

□ ▢

1 circle. ○

Circle sets of 5.

1.

2. How many sets? _____

3. How many extras? _____

4. How many buttons all together? _____

Draw 12 small triangles. Circle sets of 10.

5. How many sets of 10? _____

6. How many extras? _____

DAY 15

Write the number that comes between.

1. _____

2. _____

Look at the graph.

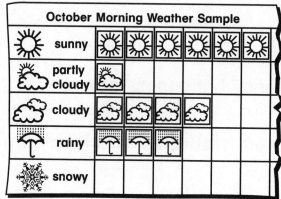

October Morning Weather Sample

3. How many days' weather are shown on the graph? _____

4. How many days would it have to rain for the rainy

days to equal the sunny days? _____

5. Are there more cloudy days or sunny days?

_____

Day 16

Make 10.

1. 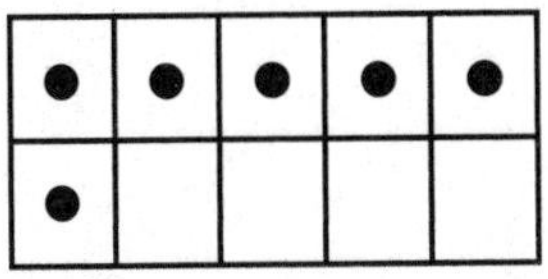

6 + ______ = 10

2. 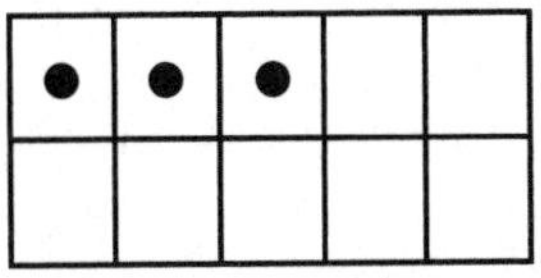

3 + ______ = 10

3. 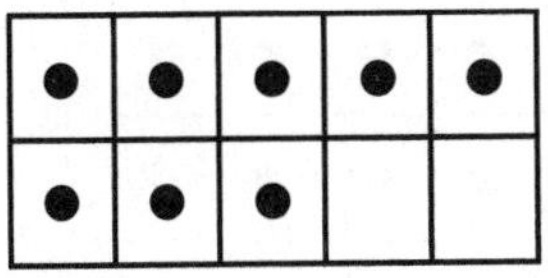

8 + ______ = 10

4. 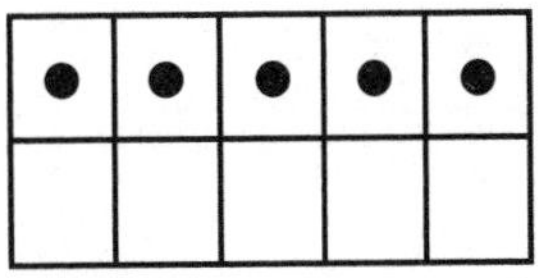

5 + ______ = 10

5. 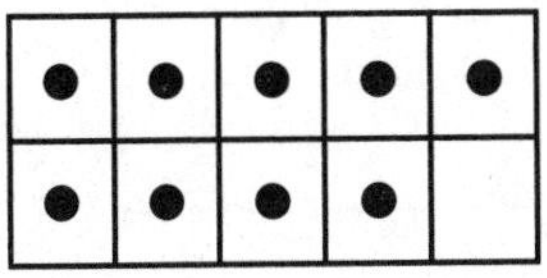

9 + ______ = 10

6. 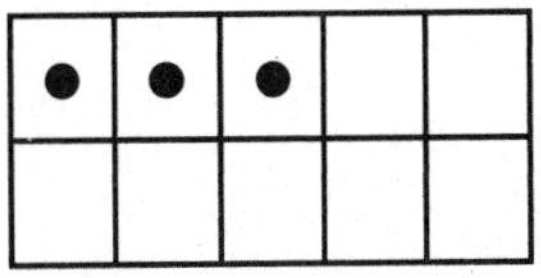

3 + ______ = 10

Make a pattern.

Use orange 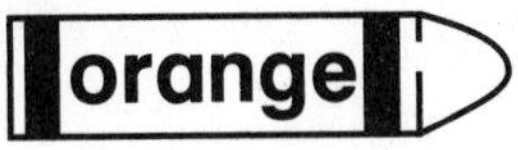

and black 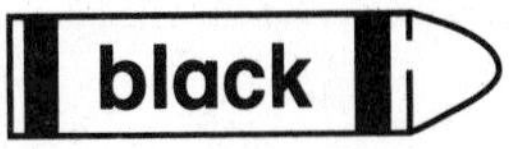

.

7. 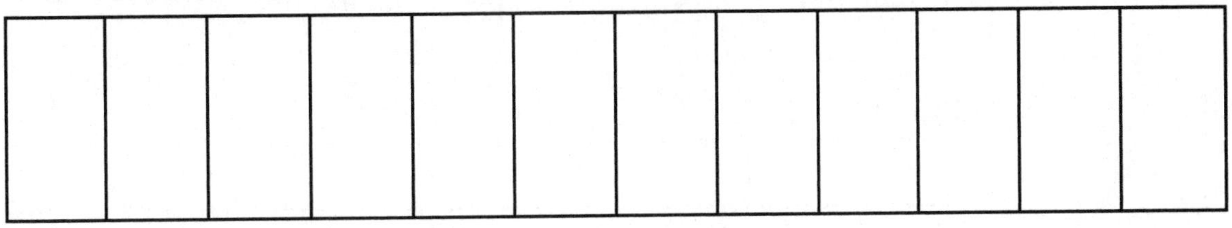

DAY 17

Add 1.

1.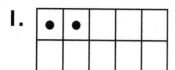

$2 + \underline{\hspace{2cm}} = \underline{\hspace{1cm}}$

2.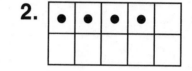

$4 + \underline{\hspace{2cm}} = \underline{\hspace{1cm}}$

3.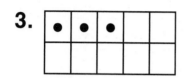

$3 + \underline{\hspace{2cm}} = \underline{\hspace{1cm}}$

4.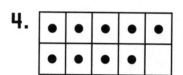

$9 + \underline{\hspace{2cm}} = \underline{\hspace{1cm}}$

5.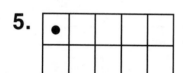

$1 + \underline{\hspace{2cm}} = \underline{\hspace{1cm}}$

6.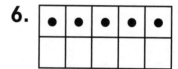

$5 + \underline{\hspace{2cm}} = \underline{\hspace{1cm}}$

Color in the shape that is shortest.

7.

8.

9.

10.

DAY 18

Draw an X on 1 dot. Subtract.

1. [grid with dots]   2. [grid with dots]   3. [grid with dots]

$2 - 1 =$ ___ $4 - 1 =$ ___ $3 - 1 =$ ___

4. [grid with dot]   5. [grid with dots]

$1 -$ ___ $=$ ___ $5 -$ ___ $=$ ___

Count the sets of 10.

6.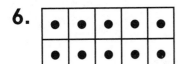

___ set $=$ ___

7.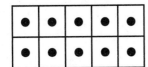

___ sets $=$ ___

8.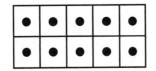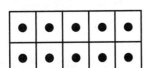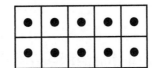

___ sets $=$ ___

DAY 19

Write the missing numbers.

1.

1	___	3	___	5	___

2.

___	12	___	14	___	16

3.

21	___	___	24	25	___

Look at the crayons.

Write how many crayons in each group.

4. ___ + ___ = ___

5. ___ + ___ = ___

6. ___ + ___ = ___

7. How many pencils all together? _____ pencils

DAY 20

Add 2.

1.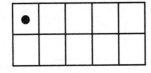

$1 + 2 =$ ____

2.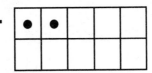

$2 + 2 =$ ____

3.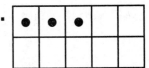

$3 + 2 =$ ____

4.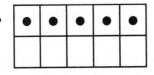

$5 + 2 =$ ____

5.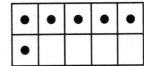

$6 + 2 =$ ____

6.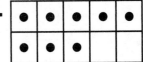

$8 + 2 =$ ____

Make 2 triangles into a square.

7.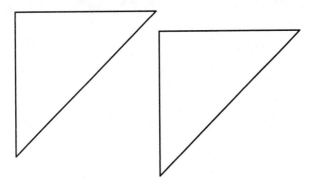

Make 4 triangles into a square.

8.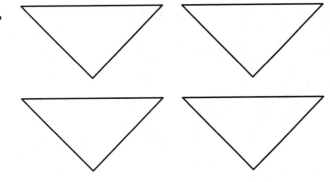

MONTHLY ASSESSMENT

Look at the Calendar.
Answer the questions.

1. If today is Friday, October 16, what was yesterday?

   Yesterday was _____

2. What will tomorrow be?

   Tomorrow will be _____

3. Color an AAAB pattern on the Calendar.
   Use an orange ┃orange┃▷ for A and
   a green ┃ **green** ┃▷ for B.

4. What numbers are in the green squares?

   ___ ___ ___ ___ ___ ___ ___ ___

MONTHLY ASSESSMENT

Fill in the numbers.

	before	after			before	after
1.	_____ 4 _____			2.	_____ 1 _____	
3.	_____ 7 _____			4.	_____ 9 _____	

Add 1.

5. $3 + \underline{\hspace{1cm}} = \underline{\hspace{1cm}}$ 6. $4 + \underline{\hspace{1cm}} = \underline{\hspace{1cm}}$

7. $0 + \underline{\hspace{1cm}} = \underline{\hspace{1cm}}$

Subtract 1.

8. $4 - \underline{\hspace{1cm}} = \underline{\hspace{1cm}}$ 9. $5 - \underline{\hspace{1cm}} = \underline{\hspace{1cm}}$

10. $1 - \underline{\hspace{1cm}} = \underline{\hspace{1cm}}$

In each row, circle dominoes to make 5.
Find 6 different ways.

11.
12.
13.
14.
15.
16.

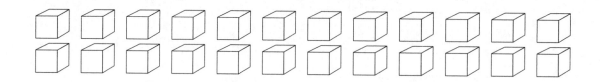

MONTHLY ASSESSMENT

Circle sets of 10.

1. How many sets? _____   2. How many extras? _____

3. Write the number all together. _____

Draw a rectangle that is shorter.

4. [   ]

Draw a triangle that is larger.

5.

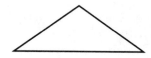

Write how many minutes.

6.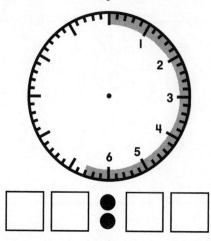

7.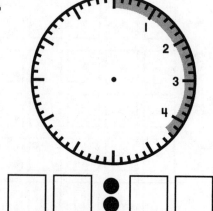

Make 5. Complete the addition sentence.

1. 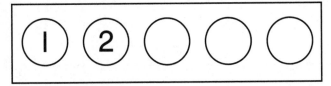   2 + ___ = 5

2.    1   ___   ___

3. 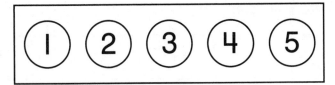   5   ___   ___

4.   1   ___   ___

Continue the patterns. Label them.

5. 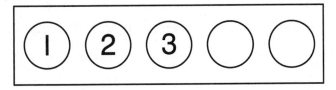 ___ ___ ___

   A ___ ___ ___ ___ ___ ___ ___ ___

6.  ___ ___ ___

   A ___ ___ ___ ___ ___ ___ ___ ___

DAY 2

Count by 5's.

1.

| 5 | 10 | ___ | ___ | ___ | ___ | 35 | ___ |

Count by 10's.

2.

| 10 | 20 | ___ | ___ | ___ | ___ | ___ |

Write the numbers between 4 and 14.

3.

| 4 | ___ | ___ | ___ | ___ | ___ | ___ | ___ | ___ | 14 |

Draw a picture of something you do before 9:00 A.M.

4.

Draw a picture of something you do after 6:00 P.M.

5.

DAY 3

Write the numbers between 4 and 26.

1.

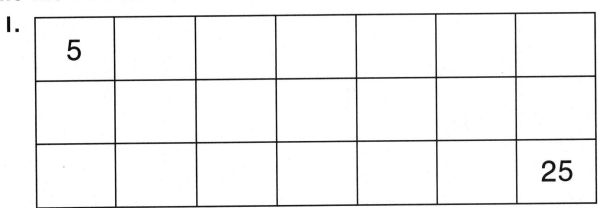

5						
						25

2. Count by 5's. Use a blue  **blue** to color
the boxes with those numbers.

Make a picture using these shapes.

3. ◯ ◯ ◯ ◯ ◯ △ ▢ ▭▭

DAY 4

Connect the objects and numbers with the same value.

1.   5   3

3¢   5¢

2.   1   4   2

2¢   4¢   1¢

Write the number.

3.

4.

5.

6.

_____¢   _____¢   _____¢   _____¢

Solve.

7. Jacob had 3 pennies.

   His mother gave him 3 more pennies.

   How many pennies does Jacob have?

_____¢ + _____¢ = _____¢

Jacob has _____ pennies.

DAY 5

Write the addition sentence.

1.
___ + ___ = ___

2.
___ + ___ = ___

3.
___ + ___ = ___

4.
___ + ___ = ___

5.
___ + ___ = ___

6.
___ + ___ = ___

Put an X in one square for each tag.

7.

8. Color the month that has the fewest birthdays green.

    What month is it? _____

9. When is your birthday? _____

Add.

1.

   2¢ + 2¢ = ___¢

2.

   2¢ + ___¢ = ___¢

3.

   ___¢ + ___¢ = ___¢

4.

   ___¢ + ___¢ = ___¢

5.

   ___¢ + ___¢ = ___¢

6.

   ___¢ + ___¢ = ___¢

Continue the pattern.

7.

   _____ _____ _____ _____ _____

8. What is the pattern?

   _____

DAY 7

**Connect the objects and numbers that
show the same number.**

1.   **2.**

TH TH   TH TH   TH TH TH   TH TH TH

TH TH   TH   TH TH TH   TH TH TH

TH   TH TH TH   TH

25   15   45   35

3. What do you notice about the clocks?

_____

Shade in 5 minutes. Add 5 minutes to each clock.

4. 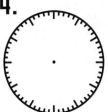 **5.**  **6.**  **7.**  **8.**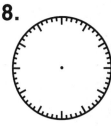

9. How many more minutes to equal half an hour?

_____

DAY 8

Draw the dots to show the addition sentence.
Write in the missing numbers.

1. $5 + \underline{} = 10$
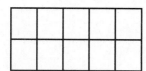

2. $9 + \underline{} = 10$
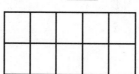

3. $4 + \underline{} = 10$
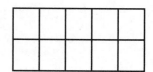

4. $2 + \underline{} = 10$
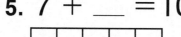

5. $7 + \underline{} = 10$

6. $3 + \underline{} = 10$
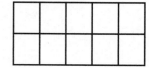

7. $8 + \underline{} = 10$
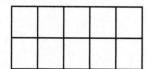

8. $1 + \underline{} = 10$
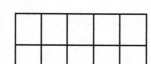

9. $0 + \underline{} = 10$
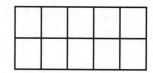

Circle sets of 10.

10.
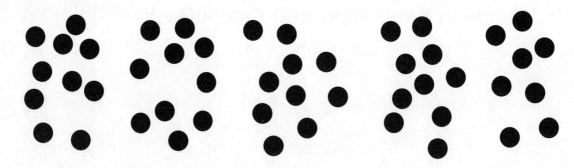

11. How many sets of 10? _____ sets of 10

12. How many extras? _____ extras

DAY 9

Circle sets of 5.

1.

2. Cut out a nickel for each set of 5 pennies.

3. Paste 1 nickel on each set of 5 pennies.

4. How many nickels can be traded for 25 pennies?

_____ nickels

Solve.

5. Alyse has 9¢.

   She gave 4 pennies to her brother Brandon.
   How much money does Alyse have left?

   $$9¢ - 4¢ = \underline{\quad\quad} ¢$$

6. Brandon had 2¢.
   Alyse gave him 4¢.
   How much money does Brandon have?

   $$\underline{\quad\quad} ¢ + \underline{\quad\quad} ¢ = \underline{\quad\quad} ¢$$

7. Can Brandon exchange pennies for a nickel?

   yes   no

Add.

1. $1 + 4 =$ _____   2. $5 + 5 =$ _____

3. $2 + 4 =$ _____   4. $4 + 5 =$ _____

Make an AABB pattern. Use ⬜**'s and** ◺**'s.**

5.

_____   _____   _____   _____   _____   _____   _____   _____

Shade in half an hour.

6. How many minutes? _____

7. How many minutes in an hour? _____

Circle sets of 10.

8.

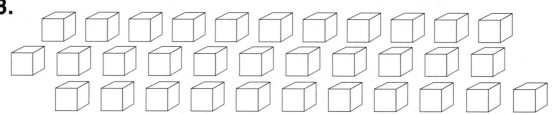

9. How many sets of 10? _____ How many extras? _____

10. Circle the number.   42   33   35   50   21

Solve.

11. Luis had 6 pennies. Maria gave him 3 more.
    How many pennies does Luis have?

$6 + 3 =$ _____ pennies

DAY 11

Add.

1.

_____¢ + _____¢ = ☐ ¢

2.

_____ + _____ = ☐ ¢

3.

_____¢ + _____¢ = ☐ ¢

4.

_____ + _____ = ☐ ¢

5. Use a yellow crayon. Color the boxes that can have 5 pennies traded for 1 nickel.

Complete the number patterns.

6. 5, 10, 15, _____, _____, _____, _____, _____, _____, _____

7. 12, 22, 32, 42, 52, _____, _____, _____, _____

8. 1, 3, 5, 7, 9, 11, _____, _____, _____

DAY 12

Cross out the pennies you could trade for a nickel.

1.

_____7_____ ¢

2.

_____ ¢

3.

_____ ¢

4.

_____ ¢

5.

_____ ¢

6.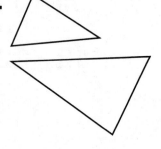

_____ ¢

Color the shape that is smaller.

7.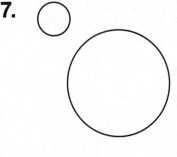

8.

9.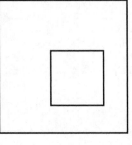

DAY 13

Match the Birthday Package to the number of its month.

1.
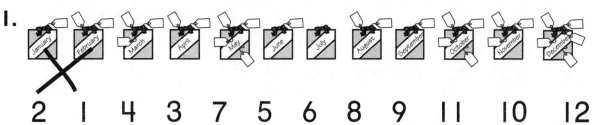

2   1   4   3   7   5   6   8   9   11   10   12

2. How many months are in a year? _____ **months**

3. Which months have you been in school?

_____

_____

4. What month is your birthday? _____

Match.

5. Triangle

It has 3 sides.

6. Square
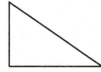

It has 4 sides.

7. Rectangle

DAY 14

Look at the Calendar. Answer the questions.

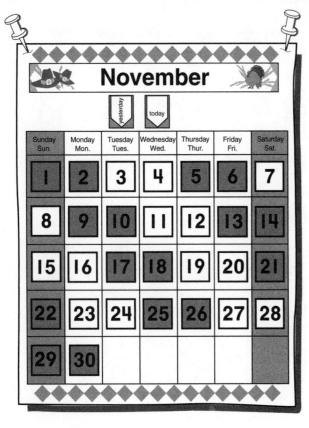

November

Sunday Sun.	Monday Mon.	Tuesday Tues.	Wednesday Wed.	Thursday Thur.	Friday Fri.	Saturday Sat.
1	2	3	4	5	6	7
8	9	10	11	12	13	14
15	16	17	18	19	20	21
22	23	24	25	26	27	28
29	30					

(yesterday, today)

1. What day does the Calendar show for today?

   _____

2. What day will tomorrow be?

   _____

3. What day was yesterday?

   _____

4. How many days are in a week?

   _____

5. What are the days of the week?

   _____

   _____

6. How many days are you in school during the week? _____

7. What day is missing?
   Wednesday, Saturday, Monday, Thursday, Sunday, Friday

   _____

DAY 15

Add.

1.

___¢ + ___¢ = ⬜ ¢

2.

___¢ + ___¢ = ⬜ ¢

3.

___¢ + ___¢ = ⬜ ¢

4.

___¢ + ___¢ = ⬜ ¢

5.

___¢ + ___¢ = ⬜ ¢

6.

___¢ + ___¢ = ⬜ ¢

Draw something to show the number 16.

Circle sets of 5.

7. How many sets? _____

8. Is 16 greater than or less than 20? _____

DAY 16

Write the missing numbers.

1.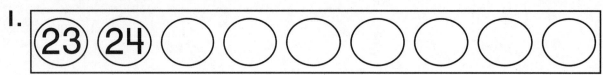

2.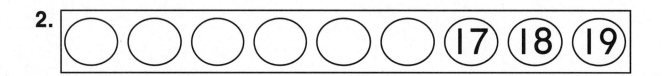

3.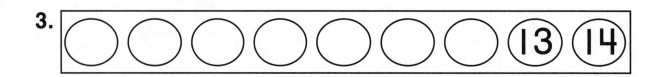

4.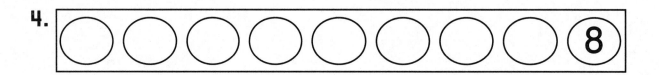

Color the patterns.

5.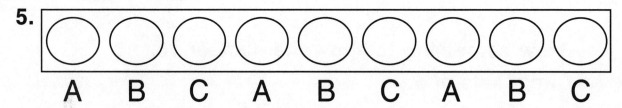

    A   B   C   A   B   C   A   B   C

6.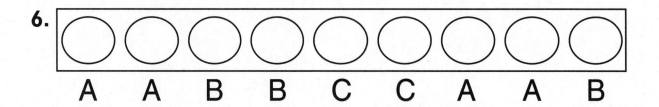

    A   A   B   B   C   C   A   A   B

DAY 17

Make 10. Write the addition sentence.

1. 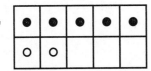   _____ + _____ = _____

2. 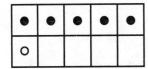   _____ + _____ = _____

3. 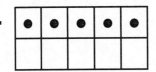   _____ + _____ = _____

4.   _____ + _____ = _____

5.   _____ + _____ = _____

Write how many clips long.

6.    _____

7. 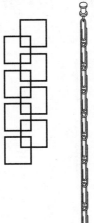   _____

8. 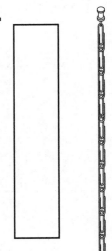   _____

DAY 18

Circle sets of 10. Write the number.

1.

_____ _____ = _____
tens ones

2.

_____ _____ = _____
tens ones

Write the number of tens and ones.

3.

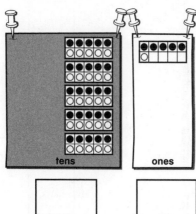

tens   ones

4.

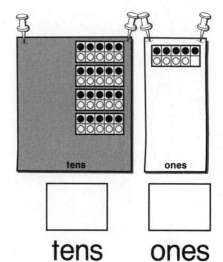

tens   ones

DAY 19

Write the missing number.

1. $2 + \underline{} = 6$ 2. $\underline{} + 4 = 6$

3. $3 + \underline{} = 8$ 4. $\underline{} + 5 = 8$

5. $4 + \underline{} = 10$ 6. $\underline{} + 6 = 10$

Solve.

7. Luis had a nickel.
   He found 3 pennies.

   How much does Luis have?

   $\underline{}¢ + \underline{}¢ = \underline{}¢$

8. Rachel had 8 cents.
   She dropped a nickel at school.

   How much does Rachel have?

   $8¢ - 5¢ = \underline{}¢$

9. Lu can trade her pennies for 1 nickel.

   How many pennies does Lu have?

   $\underline{}$ pennies

Add.

1. ||| ||||||

   3 + 7 = ____

2. |||| ||||

   5 + ____ = ____

3. |||||| ||||

   6 + ____ = ____

4. || ||||||||

   2 + ____ = ____

5. | ||||||||

   1 + ____ = ____

6. |||| ||||

   10 + ____ = ____

Solve.

7. 8 eggs are in a nest.

   4 eggs hatch, 1 egg falls down.

   How many are left? _____

8. Draw a picture to show the story.

MONTHLY ASSESSMENT

Write the numbers.

1.

			4		
					12
13					
		21			

2. Use an orange and a yellow crayon.
   Color an A A B B pattern.

3. What numbers are in the B pattern?

   _____

   _____

4. What numbers are in the A pattern?

   _____

   _____

5. What can you tell about the pattern?

   _____

   _____

MONTHLY ASSESSMENT

Add.

1. $3 + 4 =$ ___
2. $2 + 3 =$ ___
3. $4 + 5 =$ ___

4. $1 +$ ___ $= 6$
5. $4 + 4 =$ ___
6. $7 +$ ___ $= 10$

7. ___ $+ 5 = 10$
8. ___ $+ 9 = 9$
9. ___ $+ 5 = 7$

Solve.

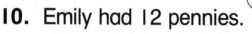

10. Emily had 12 pennies.

    She wanted to trade Tyrone for some nickels.

    How many nickels can Emily get? _____ nickels

Write the tens and ones.

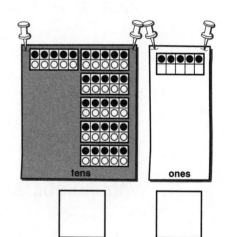

11. How many tens? _____

    How many ones? _____

    What is the number? _____

Write the addition sentence.

12.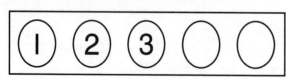

    ___ $+$ ___ $=$ ___

13.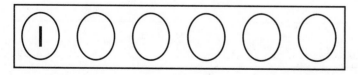

    ___ $+$ ___ $=$ ___

MONTHLY ASSESSMENT

Draw 3 different shapes that have 4 sides.

   1.

Draw a small triangle inside a large triangle.
Color the smaller triangle red.

   2.

Shade in the minutes on the clocks.

   3.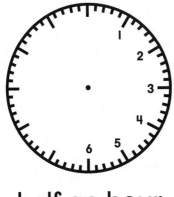

   half an hour

   4.

5. How long is an hour? _____

Cross out 1. Subtract.

1. 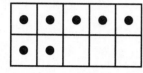   6 − 1 = _____

2.   7 − 1 = _____

3. 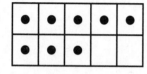   8 − 1 = _____

4. 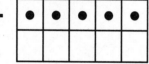   5 − 1 = _____

5. 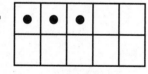   3 − 1 = _____

6. 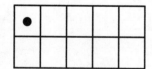   1 − _____ = _____

Color the A B B C pattern. ⟶

Use red, yellow, and blue crayons.

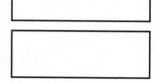
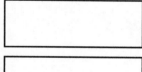
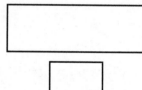
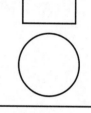
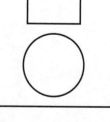
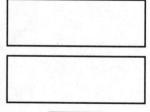

7.

DAY 2

Cross out 2. Subtract.

1.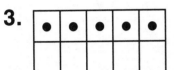

$9 - 2 = $ _____

2.

$7 - 2 = $ _____

3.

$5 - $ _____ $= $ _____

4.

_____ $- $ _____ $= $ _____

Write the addition sentences.

5.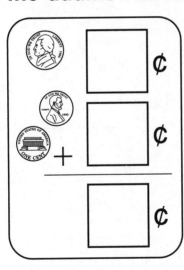

_____ ¢

_____ ¢

+

_____ ¢

6.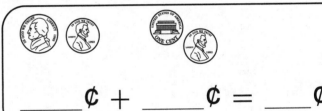

_____ ¢ $+ $ _____ ¢ $= $ _____ ¢

7.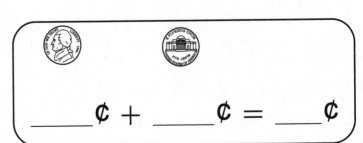

_____ ¢ $+ $ _____ ¢ $= $ _____ ¢

DAY 3

Cross out 3. Subtract.

1.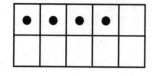

$4 - 3 = \underline{\hspace{1cm}}$

2.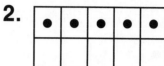

$5 - \underline{\hspace{1cm}} = \underline{\hspace{1cm}}$

3.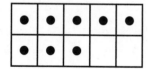

$\underline{\hspace{1cm}} - \underline{\hspace{1cm}} = \underline{\hspace{1cm}}$

4.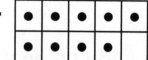

$\underline{\hspace{1cm}} - \underline{\hspace{1cm}} = \underline{\hspace{1cm}}$

5.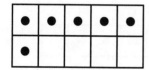

$\underline{\hspace{1cm}} - \underline{\hspace{1cm}} = \underline{\hspace{1cm}}$

6.

$\underline{\hspace{1cm}} - \underline{\hspace{1cm}} = \underline{\hspace{1cm}}$

Sort 2 ways. Draw your sort in the boxes.

7.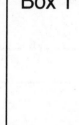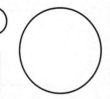

Box 1	Box 2

DAY 4

Solve the addition sentences.

Match each addition sentence to its story.

> John had 3 pennies.
> Kyle gave him 4 more pennies.
> How many pennies does
> John have?

> Conchetta had a nickel.
> She earned another nickel.
> How much money does
> Conchetta have?

1. $6 + 4 =$ _____

2. $9¢ - 5¢ =$ _____ $¢$

3. $3 + 4 =$ _____

4. $5¢ + 5¢ =$ _____ $¢$

> Matt had 9¢. He had
> a hole in his pocket
> and lost a nickel.
> How much money does
> Matt have in his pocket?

> Alex has 6 pencils.
> He has 4 more in
> his backpack.
> How many pencils does
> Alex have?

DAY 5

Add.

1. $\begin{array}{r} 3 \\ +2 \\ \hline \end{array}$
2. $\begin{array}{r} 4 \\ +4 \\ \hline \end{array}$
3. $\begin{array}{r} 5 \\ +3 \\ \hline \end{array}$
4. $\begin{array}{r} 6 \\ +4 \\ \hline \end{array}$
5. $\begin{array}{r} 7 \\ +1 \\ \hline \end{array}$

Make 10.

6.

$8 + 2 = $ _____

7.

$6 + $ _____ $ = $ _____

Make 7 as many ways as you can.

8.

_____   _____

_____   _____

_____   _____

_____

_____

_____

DAY 6

Circle sets of 5.

1.

2. How many sets of 5? _____

3. How many stamps in all? _____

4. How many more stamps to make 25? _____

5. How many more 2¢ stamps are there than 8¢ stamps?

_____

Draw an A B C pattern.
Use the stamps.

6.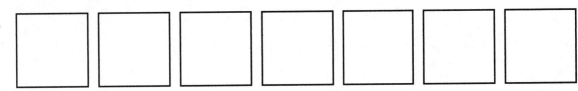

DAY 7

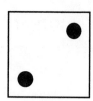 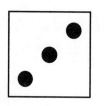 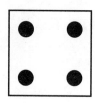

Subtract.

1. $3 - 1 =$ ___   2. $4 - 2 =$ ___   3. $5 - 3 =$ ___

4. $\begin{array}{r} 2 \\ -\ 1 \\ \hline \end{array}$ 5. $\begin{array}{r} 4 \\ -\ 3 \\ \hline \end{array}$ 6. $\begin{array}{r} 3 \\ -\ 1 \\ \hline \end{array}$

Buy each item.
Circle the coins you need.

7. 

8. 

Match.

9.    10.

 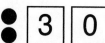

76   December

DAY 8

Write the missing numbers to make 2 sets of 10.

1.

1									10

11									20

2. What number is between 14 and 16? _____

3. What number is before 7? _____

4. What number is after 13? _____

5. What number is 3 more than 5? _____

6. What number is 6 less than 9? _____

Write the number.
Draw that number of tally marks.

	tens	ones		
	1	5	= 15	THL THL THL
7.	2	3	=	
8.	2	6	=	

DAY 9

Put an X in one square for each item.

1.

🎩 hats									
🧤 mittens									
🧥 coats									
	1	2	3	4	5	6	7	8	9

2. Are there more hats or more coats? _____

3. How many more? _____

4. How many more hats would you need to have the same amount of mittens?

   _____

5. How many children wore coats? _____ Hats? _____

DAY 10 · · · · · · · · · · · · · · · · · · CHECKPOINT

Add.

1. 5
    + 4
    ___

2. 4
    + 6
    ___

3. 7
    + 2
    ___

4. 8
    + 2
    ___

5. 3
    + 6
    ___

Subtract.

6. 5 − 3 = ___   7. 4 − 2 = ___   8. 8 − 1 = ___

Color an A B C pattern.

9.

Draw a 4-sided shape.

10.

Buy the item.
Circle the coins.

11.

DAY 11

Look at the Calendar. Answer the questions.

1. What day is between Thursday and Saturday?

   _____

2. If today is Monday, how many days until Thursday?

   _____ days

3. What days are between Friday and Tuesday?

   _____

4. What day has the most letters in it?

   _____

5. If today is December 5, how many days are there until December 8? _____ days

Complete the number patterns.

6. 15 20 25 _____ _____ _____ _____

7. 80 70 60 _____ _____ _____ _____

DAY 12

Add.

1.   (nickel) + (nickel) (penny) (penny) = _____ ¢

2. (nickel) (nickel) (nickel) + (penny) (penny) (penny) = _____ ¢

3. (nickel) (nickel) (penny) + (penny) (penny) (penny) = _____ ¢

4. (nickels) + (penny) = _____ ¢

Count the pennies.

Color the nickels that can be traded.

5.

Put an X on the shape that is longer.

Circle the shape that is shorter.

6.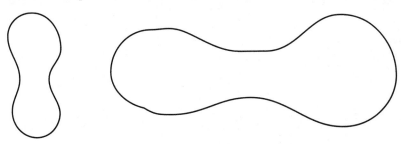

Subtract.

1. $4 - 2 =$ ___   2. $6 - $ ___ $= 3$ 3. $8 - $ ___ $= 4$

4. $10 - 5 =$ ___   5. $2 - $ ___ $= 1$ 6. $9 - 0 =$ ___

7. $\begin{array}{r} 3 \\ -3 \\ \hline \end{array}$ 8. $\begin{array}{r} 4 \\ -4 \\ \hline \end{array}$ 9. $\begin{array}{r} 5 \\ -4 \\ \hline \end{array}$ 10. $\begin{array}{r} 6 \\ -3 \\ \hline \end{array}$

Match the shapes by size.

Color the small shapes green | green |▷.

Color the large shapes blue | blue |▷.

11.

12. Are there more large shapes or small shapes?

_____

DAY 14

Subtract.

1. 6
    − 3
    ___

2. 7
    − 3
    ___

3. 8
    − 3
    ___

4. 9
    − 3
    ___

5. 5
    − 3
    ___

6. 4
    − 3
    ___

7. 3
    − 3
    ___

Solve.

8. Sam had 9 pennies. He traded with Billy for a nickel. How many pennies does he have now?

9 − ____ = ____ pennies

9. Jennifer and Sarah each have a nickel. How much money do they both have?

____ ¢ + ____ ¢ = ____ ¢

DAY 15

Add.

1. 5 +1	2. 4 +2	3. 3 +3	4. 2 +4	5. 1 +5

6. 0 +6	7. 4 +3	8. 3 +4	9. 5 +2	10. 6 +1

Circle two numbers that make 7.

Complete the addition sentence.

11. | 2 | 3 | 5 | 6 | _____ + _____ = 7

12. | 1 | 4 | 3 | 5 | _____ + _____ = 7

13. | 1 | 2 | 4 | 6 | _____ + _____ = 7

14. | 0 | 3 | 6 | 4 | _____ + _____ = 7

MONTHLY ASSESSMENT

Look at the Calendar. Answer the questions.

Sunday Sun.	Monday Mon.	Tuesday Tues.	Wednesday Wed.	Thursday Thur.	Friday Fri.	Saturday Sat.
		1	2	3	4	5
6	7	8	9	10	11	12
13	14	15	16	17	18	19
20	21	22	23	24	25	26
27	28	29	30	31		

December

yesterday ↓ today ↓

1. Color an A B C pattern with red, green, and yellow.

2. What color is it?

December 12 _____

December 29 _____

December 19 _____

3. What day of the week is it?

December 16 _____

December 7 _____

December 1 _____

MONTHLY ASSESSMENT

Add.

1. $6 + 4 = $ ___
2. $7 + 3 = $ ___
3. $8 + 1 = $ ___

4. $3 + 4 = $ ___
5. $2 + 5 = $ ___
6. $1 + 6 = $ ___

Subtract.

7. $7 - 2 = $ ___
8. $5 - 4 = $ ___
9. $4 - 4 = $ ___

10. $9 - 3 = $ ___
11. $8 - 3 = $ ___
12. $6 - 3 = $ ___

Solve.

13. Vivian, Jay, and Suzanne are going outside to play in the snow. Draw a picture of them.

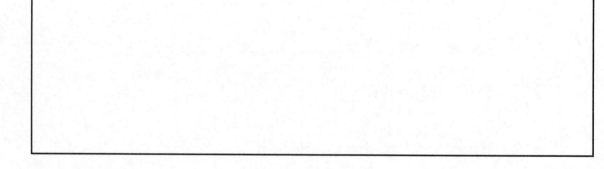

14. How many mittens will they need? _____

15. How many hats will they need? _____

16. How many coats will they need? _____

MONTHLY ASSESSMENT

Match.

1.

2.

Draw a large shape that has 4 sides.
Draw a small shape that has 4 sides.

3.

Draw a picture using shapes with 4 sides.

4.

Add.

1. $2 + 3 =$ __ 2. $3 + 4 =$ __ 3. $4 + 5 =$ __

4. $2 + 1 =$ __ 5. $3 + 1 =$ __ 6. $4 + 1 =$ __

7. $\begin{array}{r} 3 \\ + 3 \\ \hline \end{array}$ 8. $\begin{array}{r} 6 \\ + 2 \\ \hline \end{array}$ 9. $\begin{array}{r} 9 \\ + 1 \\ \hline \end{array}$ 10. $\begin{array}{r} 1 \\ + 8 \\ \hline \end{array}$

Complete the patterns.

Color them.

11.

A A B B A A B B __ __ __ __

12.

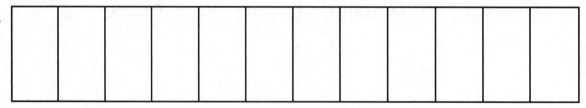

A B C A B C __ __ __ __ __ __

DAY 2

Write the addition sentence.

1.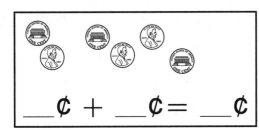
__¢ + __¢ = __¢

2.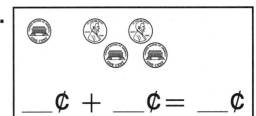
__¢ + __¢ = __¢

3.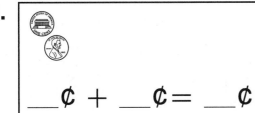
__¢ + __¢ = __¢

4.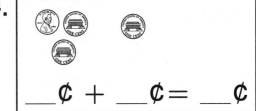
__¢ + __¢ = __¢

5.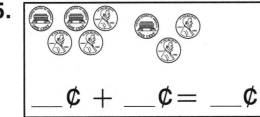
__¢ + __¢ = __¢

6.
__¢ + __¢ = __¢

7. Color the squares yellow where a nickel can be traded.

Circle sets of 7¢.

8.

9. How many sets? _____ sets

DAY 3

Add 2.

1. 8
   +2

2. 6
   +2

3. 4
   +2

4. 2
   +2

5. 0
   +2

Add 3.

6. 1
   +3

7. 3
   +3

8. 5
   +3

9. 7
   +3

10. 0
    +3

Color triangles blue,
squares green,
and circles orange.

11.

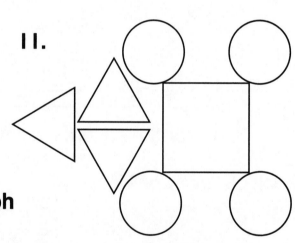

Color one square on the graph
for each shape found above.

12.

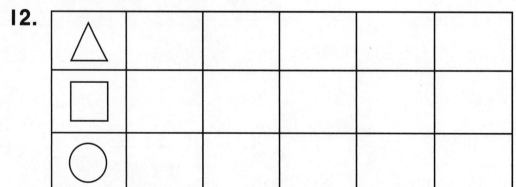

13. Which shape is used the least? _____

DAY 4

Cross out 2. Subtract.

1. $8¢ - 2¢ = 6¢$

2.   ___¢ − ___¢ = ___¢

3.   ___¢ − ___¢ = ___¢

4.   ___¢ − ___¢ = ___¢

5.   ___¢ − ___¢ = ___¢

Look at the Birthday Boxes.

6. What month is 2 months before August? _____

7. What month is 2 months after August? _____

8. What is the first month of the year? _____

9. What month has 5 birthdays? _____

10. What month has 2 fewer birthdays? _____

Add.

1.  $5¢ + 3¢ = 8¢$

2.  $\_\_¢ + \_\_¢ = \_\_¢$

3.  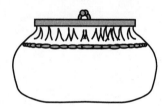 $\_\_¢ + \_\_¢ = \_\_¢$

4. $\_\_¢ + \_\_¢ = \_\_¢$

There is 7¢ in the purse. Put an X on the coins.

5.

Put an X on the coins that could be used to make 14¢.
Find 3 ways.

6.

7.

8.

DAY 6

Write the addition sentence.

1. ● ● ● ○ ○ ○ ○ ○ ○ ○

2. ● ● ● ● ○ ○ ○ ○ ○ ○   ___ + ___ = 10

3. ● ○ ○ ○ ○ ○ ○ ○ ○ ○   ___ + ___ = 10

4. ● ● ● ● ● ● ● ● ● ○   _____ = 10

5. ● ● ● ● ● ● ● ● ○ ○   _____ = 10

6. ● ● ● ● ● ● ● ○ ○ ○   _____

Label the pattern.

7.

___ ___ ___ ___ ___ ___ ___ ___ ___ ___

Make your own AABBB pattern.

8.

DAY 7

Circle sets of 5.

1.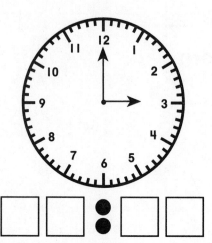

2. **How many sets of 5?** _____

3. **Count by 5's.**

   5   10 _____ _____ _____ _____

Look at the clocks.

Write the time.

4.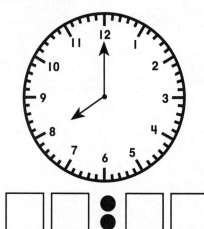

5.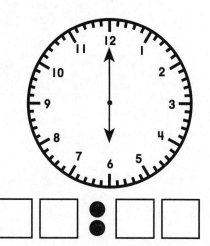

6.

7.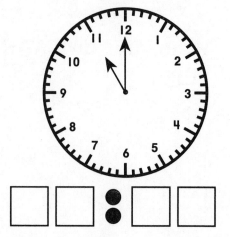

DAY 8

Count the tens and the ones. Write the number.

1.

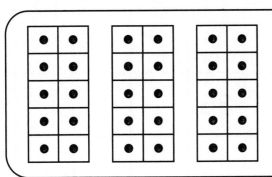

tens ones =

2.

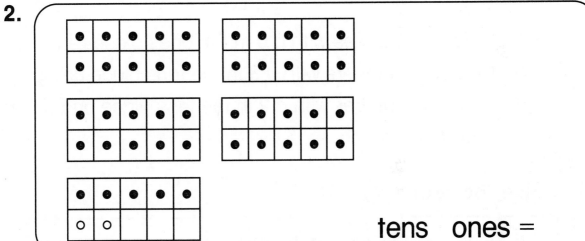

tens ones =

Draw snowflakes to show 2 tens and 3 ones.

3.

Write the missing numbers.

1.

21									
				35					

2. Color the squares with a 0 in the ones place red.

3. Color the numbers with a 3 in the tens place orange.

4. Color the number with a 2 in the tens place and a 7 in the ones place green.

Solve the problems.

5. Five cookies were in the bag. Joshua ate 2 for lunch.

   How many are left? _____ cookies

   Write the number sentence. _____ − _____ = _____

6. Antonio found 4 rocks. Carmen gave him 2 rocks.

   Nye gave him 3 rocks.

   How many rocks does Antonio have now? _____ rocks

   Write the number sentence. _____ + _____ + _____ = _____

DAY 10 CHECKPOINT

Add.

1. $\begin{array}{r} 6 \\ + 2 \\ \hline \end{array}$
2. $\begin{array}{r} 6 \\ + 4 \\ \hline \end{array}$
3. $\begin{array}{r} 5 \\ + 3 \\ \hline \end{array}$
4. $\begin{array}{r} 7 \\ + 2 \\ \hline \end{array}$
5. $\begin{array}{r} 4 \\ + 6 \\ \hline \end{array}$
6. $\begin{array}{r} 2 \\ + 8 \\ \hline \end{array}$

Subtract.

7. $6¢ - 4¢ = \underline{\hspace{1cm}}¢$ 8. $8¢ - 6¢ = \underline{\hspace{1cm}}¢$

Circle sets of 10.

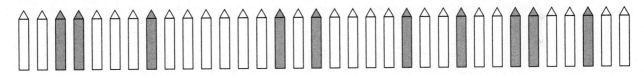

9. How many sets of ten? _____ How many ones? _____
   How many all together ? _____

Write the time.

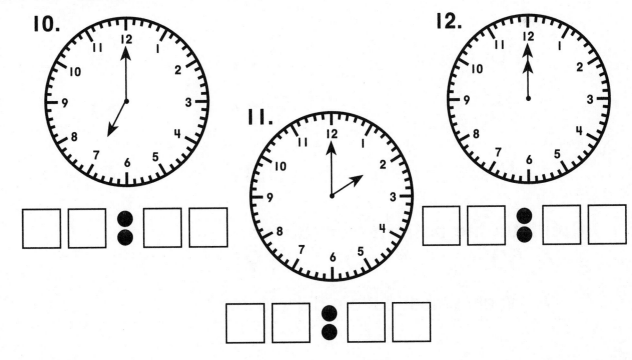

10.   11.   12.

DAY 11

Color each set of ten a different color.

1.
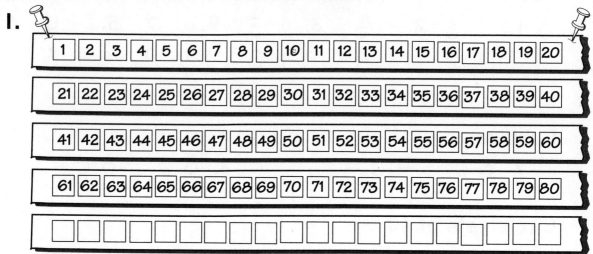

2. How many more sets of 10 to get to 100? _____ sets

Write the missing numbers.

3. After	4. Before	5. Between
10, ___	___, 51	44, ___, 46
20, ___	___, 61	54, ___, 56
30, ___	___, 71	64, ___, 66
40, ___	___, 81	74, ___, 76

Continue the pattern from above.

6. 50, ___   7. ___, 91   8. ___, ___, ___

9. What number pattern did you see?

_____

DAY 12

Circle 10¢. Cut and glue a dime on each set of 10¢.

1.

Connect the same.

2.   1¢   5¢   10¢

Add.

3.

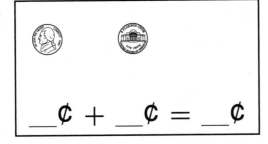

____¢ + ___¢ = ___¢

4.

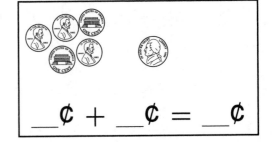

____¢ + ___¢ = ___¢

DAY 13

Circle sets that can be traded for a dime.

1.

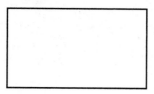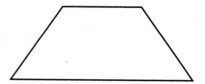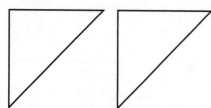

2. _____ sets can be traded.

Draw a shape with 3 sides below each shape with 4 sides.

3.

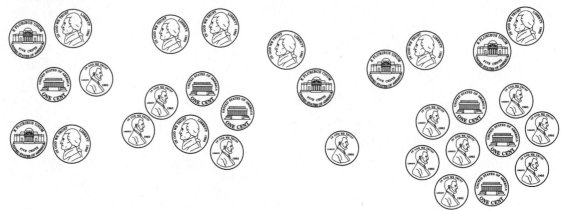

Make a square using 2 triangles.

4.

DAY 14

Add.

1. $5 + 5 = \underline{\hspace{1.5cm}}$

2. $7 + 3 = \underline{\hspace{1.5cm}}$

3. $6 + 4 = \underline{\hspace{1.5cm}}$

4. $2 + 8 = \underline{\hspace{1.5cm}}$

5. $8 + \underline{\hspace{1.5cm}} = 10$

6. $3 + \underline{\hspace{1.5cm}} = 10$

7. $4 + \underline{\hspace{1.5cm}} = 10$

8. $5 + \underline{\hspace{1.5cm}} = 10$

9. $10 + \underline{\hspace{1.5cm}} = 10$

10. $0 + \underline{\hspace{1.5cm}} = 10$

Look at the Birthday Boxes.

11. Which months are missing?

_____ _____ _____

_____ _____

12. A new year begins this month. What month is it?

_____

13. We have Thanksgiving during month 11. What month is it?

_____

DAY 15

Write the number sentence.

1.  $5 - 2 =$ ___

2.  ___ $-$ ___ $=$ ___

3.  ___ $-$ ___ $=$ ___

4.  ___ $-$ ___ $=$ ___

There are 4 coins that are worth 17¢ in the bank.
Put an X on them.

5.

Find 2 ways to make 21¢.
Put an X on the coins.

6.

7.

DAY 16

Write the number sentence.

1.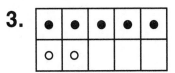

___ + ___ = ___

2.

___ + ___ = ___

3.

___ + ___ = ___

4.

___ + ___ = ___

5.

___ + ___ = ___

6.

___ + ___ = ___

7.

___ − ___ = ___

8.

10 − ___ = ___

9.

7 − ___ = ___

10.

___ − ___ = ___

11.

___ − ___ = ___

12.

___ − ___ = ___

Continue the pattern.

13.

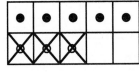   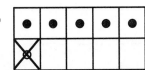 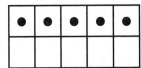 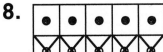 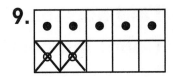

_____   _____   _____   _____   _____   _____

DAY 17

Subtract.

1. 5
   − 4

2. 4
   − 3

3. 3
   − 2

4. 2
   − 1

5. 5
   − 3

6. 4
   − 2

7. 3
   − 1

8. 2
   − 0

Find how long.

Count the coins.

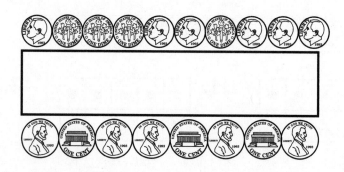

9. _____ pennies = _____ ¢

10. _____ dimes = _____ ¢

DAY 18

Circle sets of 10.

1.

2. Count tens and ones. Write the number.

_____   _____ = _____

tens   **ones**

Circle sets of 10.

3.

4. Count tens and ones. Write the number.

_____   _____ = _____

tens   **ones**

Draw a picture to show the number.

5.

2 tens   3 ones

DAY 19

Draw an X in a square for each one.

1.

Solve.

2. If all the dimes were in a box,
how many dimes would be there? _____
How much are they worth? _____ ¢

3. If all the nickels were in a box,
how many nickels would be there? _____
How much are they worth? _____ ¢

4. If all the pennies were in a box,
how many pennies would be there? _____
How much are they worth? _____ ¢

DAY 20

Add.

1.	2.	3.	4.	5.	6.
6 + 1	4 + 1	2 + 2	5 + 2	2 + 0	1 + 6

7.	8.	9.	10.	11.	12.
7 + 2	5 + 2	9 + 1	3 + 3	2 + 3	5 + 2

Find the answers.

1	2	3	4	5	6	7	8	9	10
11	12	13	14	15	16	17	18	19	20
21	22	23	24	25	26	27	28	29	30
31	32	33	34	35	36	37	38	39	40

13. Put an X on every 5th square.

14. Color every 7th square green.

15. Draw a circle in every 3rd square.

16. What squares are covered more than once?

_____ _____ _____ _____

MONTHLY ASSESSMENT

Use the Calendar.

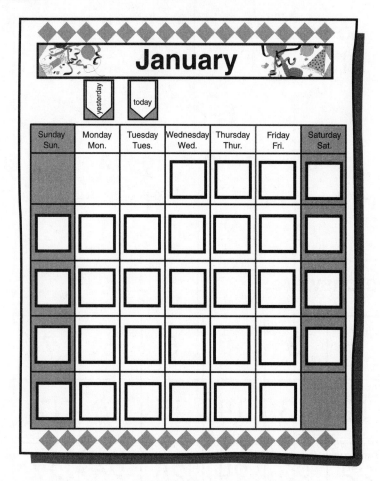

1. Fill in the dates on the Calendar. Begin with 1 on Wednesday.

2. Color in an AAB pattern. Use blue for A and white for B.

3. What numbers are in the white squares?

   _____

4. What day is the 28th? _____

5. What color is the 8th? _____

MONTHLY ASSESSMENT

Add.

1. 6
  + 2

2. 9
  + 1

3. 10
  + 0

4. 2
  + 8

5. 5
  + 3

6. 3
  + 6

Subtract.

7. $5 - 3 = $ ___   8. $2 - 0 = $ ___   9. $4 - 1 = $ ___

10. $3 - 2 = $ ___   11. $5 - 2 = $ ___   12. $4 - 2 = $ ___

Solve the problem.

13. Jessie had 2 nickels and 1 penny.

   How much money did Jessie have? _____ ¢

   Write the number sentence.

   _____

Draw the coins. Show 3 ways to make 10¢.

14.

15.

16.

MONTHLY ASSESSMENT

Write the time.

1.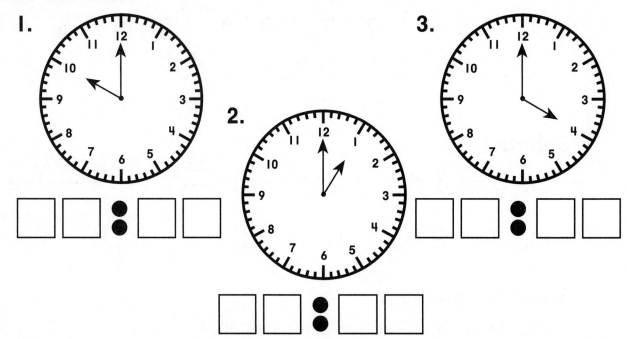

2.

3.

Make a rectangle using 4 triangles. Show 2 ways.

4. 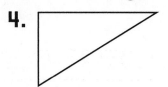   or

Shade in how many minutes in an hour.
Use a yellow crayon.

5.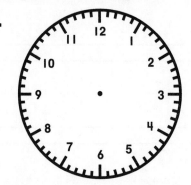

6. How many minutes are in an hour? _____

Subtract.

1. $6 - 2 = $ _____

2. $4 - 1 = $ _____

3. $7 - 4 = $ _____

4. $8 - 5 = $ _____

5. $10 - 6 = $ _____

6. $8 - 4 = $ _____

7. $9 - 6 = $ _____

8. $10 - 4 = $ _____

9. $5 - 2 = $ _____

10. Draw a rectangle around all the answers greater than 5.

11. Circle the answers that are between 3 and 5.

12. Write a number sentence that has a difference of 7.

$$\text{\_\_\_\_} - \text{\_\_\_\_} = 7$$

Make a pattern.

13.

14. Describe the pattern.

_____

_____

DAY 2

Subtract.

1. 8
    − 6

2. 6
    − 2

3. 7
    − 4

4. 5
    − 1

5. 9
    − 7

6. 10
    − 8

7. 6
    − 5

8. 9
    − 7

9. 7
    − 5

10. 8
    − 6

11. Circle all the answers that are less than 4.

Draw larger and smaller shapes.

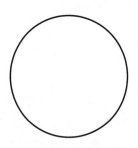

12. Draw a larger square around the circle.

13. Draw a smaller triangle inside the circle.

DAY 3

Add.

1.	2.	3.	4.	5.
2 + 4	5 + 3	6 + 3	1 + 3	6 + 4

6.	7.	8.	9.	10.
7 + 2	7 + 3	7 + 1	2 + 5	4 + 3

11. 2 + 3 = _____   12. 4 + 4 = _____

13. Circle the answers greater than 8.

14. Draw a rectangle around the answers less than 5.

Circle the shape that is the same.

15.

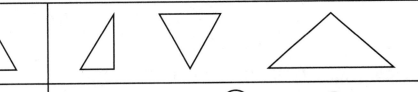

16.

17.

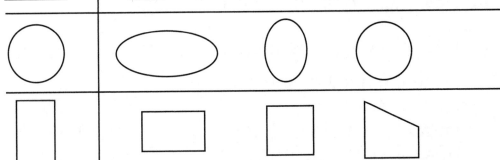

DAY 4

Look at the tags for both months.
Write an addition sentence.

1. February + August $2 + 2 = 4$

2. June + November   ___ + ___ = ___

3. May + October   ___ + ___ = ___

4. December + January   ___ + ___ = ___

5. March + July   ___ + ___ = ___

6. September + April   ___ + ___ = ___

7. It is February. Hannah has a birthday in September. How many months does she have to wait until her birthday?

    _____ months

8. How many birthdays are in the year? _____

9. How many more birthdays does December have than April? Write the number sentence. _____ — _____ = _____

10. How many more birthdays does October have than May? Write the number sentence. _____ — _____ = _____

DAY 5

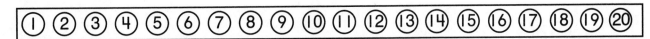

① ② ③ ④ ⑤ ⑥ ⑦ ⑧ ⑨ ⑩ ⑪ ⑫ ⑬ ⑭ ⑮ ⑯ ⑰ ⑱ ⑲ ⑳

Add. You may use the number line above.

1. $8 + 2 = \underline{\hspace{1cm}}$

2. $10 + 2 = \underline{\hspace{1cm}}$

3. $12 + 2 = \underline{\hspace{1cm}}$

4. $14 + 2 = \underline{\hspace{1cm}}$

5. $16 + 2 = \underline{\hspace{1cm}}$

6. $18 + 2 = \underline{\hspace{1cm}}$

7. $3 + 3 = \underline{\hspace{1cm}}$

8. $6 + 3 = \underline{\hspace{1cm}}$

9. $9 + 3 = \underline{\hspace{1cm}}$

Write as many number sentences for 8 as you can.

10. $1 + 7 = 8$

11. $10 - 2 = 8$

DAY 6

Subtract.

1. $\begin{array}{r} 5¢ \\ -\ 5¢ \\ \hline ¢ \end{array}$	2. $\begin{array}{r} 10¢ \\ -\ 8¢ \\ \hline ¢ \end{array}$	3. $\begin{array}{r} 6¢ \\ -\ 5¢ \\ \hline ¢ \end{array}$	4. $\begin{array}{r} 3¢ \\ -\ 1¢ \\ \hline ¢ \end{array}$
5. $\begin{array}{r} 9¢ \\ -\ 7¢ \\ \hline ¢ \end{array}$	6. $\begin{array}{r} 6¢ \\ -\ 5¢ \\ \hline ¢ \end{array}$	7. $\begin{array}{r} 7¢ \\ -\ 3¢ \\ \hline ¢ \end{array}$	8. $\begin{array}{r} 8¢ \\ -\ 3¢ \\ \hline ¢ \end{array}$

Continue the pattern.

9.

_____ _____ _____ _____ _____

10. What do you notice about the pattern?

_____

DAY 7

Add 5.

1.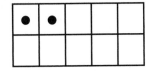

$$2 + 5 = 7$$

2.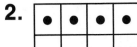

__ + __ = __

3.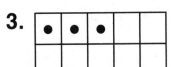

__ + __ = __

4.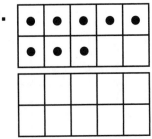

__ + __ = __

5.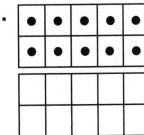

__ + __ = __

6.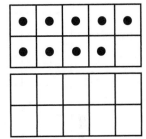

__ + __ = __

Write the time.

7.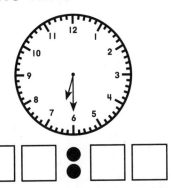

8.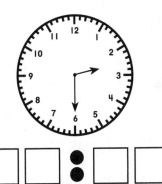

Draw the hands on the clocks.

9.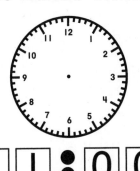

1 1 : 0 0

10.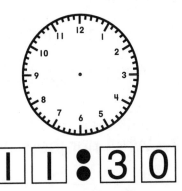

1 1 : 3 0

DAY 8

Add.

1. $9 + 5 =$ _____   2. $6 + 8 =$ _____   3. $7 + 7 =$ _____

Write the missing numbers.

4.

1									
			14						
	22								
					36				
									50

5. What number has 5 ones and 3 tens? _____

6. What numbers have a 7 in the ones place?

_____

7. What number has 3 tens and 3 ones? _____

8. What numbers do not have a number in the tens place?

_____

9. What numbers have a 0 in the ones place?

_____

DAY 9

Connect the same.

1.

8 + 5   14

2.

10 + 4   13

3.

9 + 6   16

4.

6 + 10   15

Solve the problems. Write the number sentence.

5. Arrie had 7 crackers. She ate 2. How many crackers does Arrie have now? _____ crackers   7 ◯ __ = __

6. Katie gave Arrie 5 more crackers. How many crackers does she have now? _____ crackers   5 ◯ __ = __

Add.

1.   5
    + 7
    _____

2.   6
    + 6
    _____

3.   3
    + 8
    _____

4.   8
    + 5
    _____

Subtract.

5.   10
    − 4
    _____

6.   6
    − 3
    _____

7.   9
    − 5
    _____

8.   5
    − 2
    _____

Write the time.

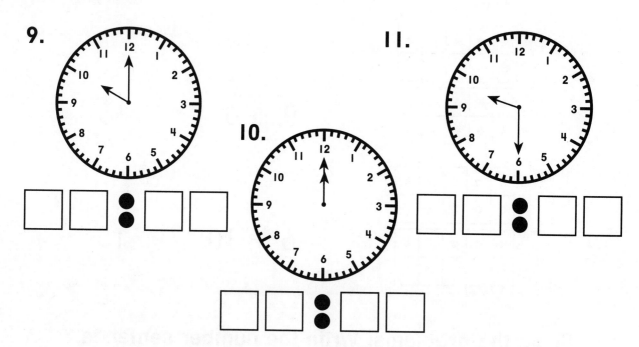

9.

10.

11.

Make and label a pattern with 3 types of buttons.

12.

_____ _____ _____ _____ _____ _____ _____ _____

DAY 11

Add.

1. 5¢ + 10¢ = __¢   2. 20¢ + 5¢ = __¢

3. 15¢ + 10¢ = __¢   4. 10¢ + 15¢ = __¢

5. 15¢ + 15¢ = __¢   6. 10¢ + 10¢ = __¢

7. 10¢ + 5¢ = __¢   8. 5¢ + 5¢ = __¢

Write the number patterns.

9. _20_ _25_ _30_ ___ ___ ___ ___

10. _1_ _3_ _5_ ___ ___ ___ ___

11. _2_ _4_ _6_ ___ ___ ___ ___

12. Describe the 3rd pattern.

_____

DAY 12

Trade for the fewest coins. Put an X on the coins.

1. 12¢

2. 14¢

3. 9¢

4. 21¢

5. 17¢

Using the fewest coins, write how many nickels and dimes.

	Money	nickels	dimes
6.	15¢		
7.	25¢		
8.	45¢		
9.	5¢		

DAY 13

Write the missing numbers.

1. ◯ ◯ ◯ ◯ (83) (84)

2. ◯ ◯ (70) ◯ ◯ ◯

3. ◯ ◯ (99) ◯ ◯ ◯

4. ◯ ◯ ◯ ◯ (50) ◯

5. ◯ ◯ ◯ ◯ ◯ (100)

6. Color any circle with a 0 in the ones place yellow.

7. Color any circle with an 8 in the ones place green.

8. Color any circle with a 2 in the ones place orange.

9. Color any circle with a 6 in the ones place red.

Write the number of triangles.

10. 　＿＿＿＿ triangles

DAY 14

Add.

1. $10¢ + 5¢ + 1¢ + 1¢ + 1¢ + 1¢ = \underline{\hspace{1cm}}¢$

2. $10¢ + 10¢ + 1¢ + 1¢ = \underline{\hspace{1cm}}¢$

3. $5¢ + 5¢ + 5¢ + 1¢ + 1¢ + 1¢ = \underline{\hspace{1cm}}¢$

4. $10¢ + 5¢ + 1¢ + 1¢ = \underline{\hspace{1cm}}¢$

Solve.

5. Sheyann found 2 nickels in her backpack. How much money does she have?

   $\underline{\hspace{1cm}}¢ + \underline{\hspace{1cm}}¢ = \underline{\hspace{1cm}}¢$

6. Mario has enough pennies to trade for a dime and a nickel. How much money does he have?

   $\underline{\hspace{1cm}}¢ + \underline{\hspace{1cm}}¢ = \underline{\hspace{1cm}}¢$

DAY 15

Subtract.

1. 7
   − 0
   ___

2. 8
   − 2
   ___

3. 10
   − 4
   ___

4. 7
   − 1
   ___

5. 8
   − 6
   ___

6. 10
   − 1
   ___

7. 9
   − 5
   ___

8. 7
   − 2
   ___

9. 9
   − 7
   ___

10. 10
   − 5
   ___

11. 8
   − 5
   ___

12. 7
   − 6
   ___

Write 5 ways to make 20¢.
Use dimes, nickels,
and pennies.

13.		
14.		
15.		
16.		
17.		

DAY 16

How many? Write the number.

1.
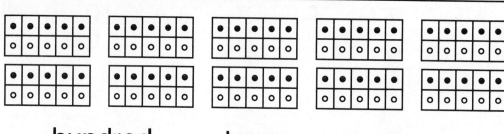

   __ hundred   __ tens   __ ones = __

2.
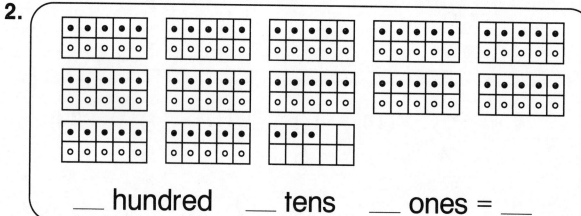

   __ hundred   __ tens   __ ones = __

3.
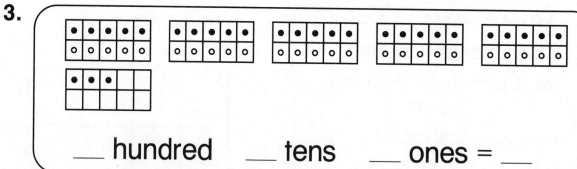

   __ hundred   __ tens   __ ones = __

Make an ABBC pattern.

4.

DAY 17

Add dots to make 64.

1.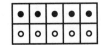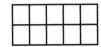

  _____ more

2.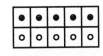

 _____ more

3.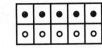

_____ more

Draw the hands to show the time.

4.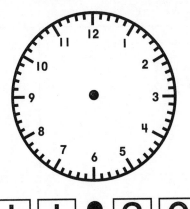

1 1 : 3 0

5.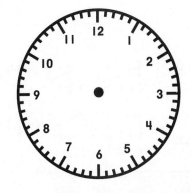

☐ 3 : 0 0

DAY 18

Add.

1. $\begin{array}{r} 8 \\ +4 \\ \hline \end{array}$ 2. $\begin{array}{r} 7 \\ +5 \\ \hline \end{array}$ 3. $\begin{array}{r} 5 \\ +7 \\ \hline \end{array}$ 4. $\begin{array}{r} 6 \\ +8 \\ \hline \end{array}$ 5. $\begin{array}{r} 9 \\ +5 \\ \hline \end{array}$ 6. $\begin{array}{r} 4 \\ +8 \\ \hline \end{array}$

Draw tally marks to find the answer.

7. $5 + 12$
   卌 ||

8. $6 + 13$

9. $4 + 13$

10. $8 + 13$

Circle sets of 10. Write the number.

	tens	ones	equal
11. 卌 卌 卌 卌 卌			
12. 卌 卌 卌 卌 卌 卌 卌 卌 ||||			
13. 卌 卌 卌 卌 卌 卌 卌 ||			

DAY 19

Write the numbers in order.

1. 57, 55, 58, 56 _____

2. 73, 71, 72, 74 _____

3. 98, 100, 101, 99 _____

4. 36, 35, 34, 33 _____

Solve.

5. Rudy has 21¢ in his pocket. He has 3 coins. What are they?

_____

6. Sherise wants to buy a butterfly stamp
   and a happy face stamp.
   How much does Sherise need?

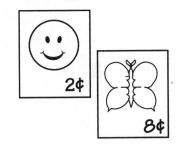

7. Manny saw 10 bears at the zoo.
   Emily saw 8 bears.
   How many more bears
   did Manny see than Emily? _____ more bears

DAY 20

Circle even or odd.

1.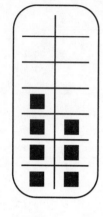

even   odd

2.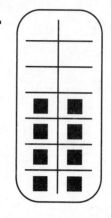

even   odd

3.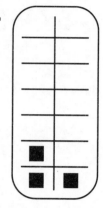

even   odd

4.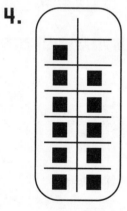

even   odd

5.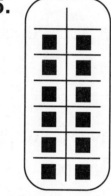

even   odd

6.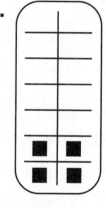

even   odd

Put the numbers in the odd box or even box.

3   4   6   7   10   11   13   14   18   19   22   23

7.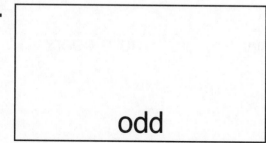

odd

8.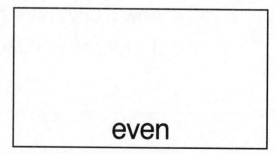

even

MONTHLY ASSESSMENT

Look at the Calendar. Answer the questions.

1. What shape will 24 be?

   _____

2. What shape will 21 be?

   _____

3. Complete the pattern.

4. What numbers are hearts?

   1, 3, 5, _____

5. What do you notice about the Calendar pattern?

   _____

   _____

MONTHLY ASSESSMENT

Add.

1. 3
   +5
   ___

2. 4
   +4
   ___

3. 0
   +6
   ___

4. 7
   +2
   ___

5. 5
   +4
   ___

6. 8
   +5
   ___

7. 7
   +7
   ___

8. 5
   +6
   ___

9. 9
   +4
   ___

10. 6
    +8
    ___

Subtract.

11. $5 - 3 =$ _____

12. $6 - 4 =$ _____

13. $8 - 5 =$ _____

14. $10 - 2 =$ _____

15. $7 - 3 =$ _____

16. $8 - 8 =$ _____

Solve.

17. Michael had 2 yo-yos. He lost 1 on the way to school.

    How many yo-yos does he have now? _____ yo-yo

18. You have 12¢ in your pocket.
    Put an X on the coins you have.

MONTHLY ASSESSMENT

Write the time.

1.
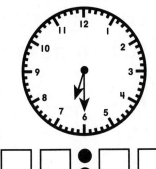

☐ ☐ : ☐ ☐

2.

☐ ☐ : ☐ ☐

3.

☐ ☐ : ☐ ☐

Draw the hands to show the time.

4.
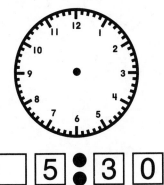

☐ 5 : 3 0

5.

☐ 8 : 3 0

6.
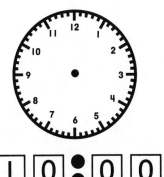

1 0 : 0 0

Make a picture with 6 triangles and 1 circle.

7.

Add. Circle odd or even.

Draw the number of mittens you add each time.

19			20
17			18
15			16
18			14
11			12
9			10
7	🧤		8
5	🧤	🧤	6
3	🧤	🧤	4
1	🧤	🧤	2

1. Add 1 more mitten.

   $7 + \underline{\qquad} = \underline{\qquad}$

   odd   even

2. Add 3 more mittens.

   $\underline{\qquad} + \underline{\qquad} = \underline{\qquad}$

   odd   even

3. Add 2.

   $\underline{\qquad} + \underline{\qquad} = \underline{\qquad}$

   odd   even

4. Add 5.

   $\underline{\qquad} + \underline{\qquad} = \underline{\qquad}$

   odd   even

5. Add 2.

   $\underline{\qquad} + \underline{\qquad} = \underline{\qquad}$

   odd   even

Complete the pattern.

6.    _____ _____ _____

DAY 2

Connect the same.

1.

 25¢   10¢   5¢

Add.
Color boxes where you can trade for a quarter yellow.

2.   _____ ¢

3.   _____ ¢

4.   _____ ¢

5.   _____ ¢

6.   _____ ¢

7. _____ ¢

DAY 3

Add.

1.	3	2.	10	3.	16	4.	4	5.	12
	+ 11		+ 8		+ 3		+ 13		+ 6

6.	14	7.	6	8.	19	9.	5	10.	11
	+ 3		+7		+ 0		+2		+ 7

11. Circle even answers.

12. Draw a rectangle around odd answers.

Look at the shapes.

Draw a line down the middle of each shape.

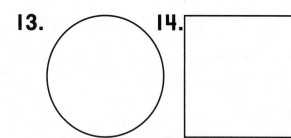 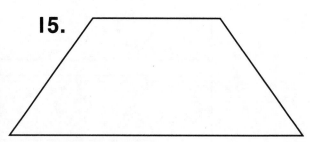

13.   14.   15.

16. Color the left half of each shape red.

17. Color the right half of each shape blue.

DAY 4

Add.

1. $\begin{array}{r} 3 \\ +6 \\ \hline \end{array}$ 2. $\begin{array}{r} 13 \\ +\ 6 \\ \hline \end{array}$ 3. $\begin{array}{r} 4 \\ +6 \\ \hline \end{array}$ 4. $\begin{array}{r} 14 \\ +\ 6 \\ \hline \end{array}$

5. $\begin{array}{r} 6 \\ +3 \\ \hline \end{array}$ 6. $\begin{array}{r} 16 \\ +\ 3 \\ \hline \end{array}$ 7. $\begin{array}{r} 7 \\ +3 \\ \hline \end{array}$ 8. $\begin{array}{r} 17 \\ +\ 3 \\ \hline \end{array}$

Solve. Write the number sentence.

9. Autumn had 8 crayons in a box. She put 4 crayons on the table. How many crayons are still in the box? $\underline{\ 8\ } - \underline{\ 4\ } = \underline{\quad}$

10. Lucas has 6 pencils. Debbie has 3. How many more pencils does Lucas have than Debbie? $\underline{\quad} - \underline{\quad} = \underline{\quad}$

11. Pete has 7 toy cars. Fred has 6. How many toy cars do they have all together? $\underline{\quad} + \underline{\quad} = \underline{\quad}$

DAY 5

Subtract.

1. $\begin{array}{r} 10 \\ -\ 5 \\ \hline \end{array}$
2. $\begin{array}{r} 9 \\ -3 \\ \hline \end{array}$
3. $\begin{array}{r} 8 \\ -5 \\ \hline \end{array}$
4. $\begin{array}{r} 6 \\ -4 \\ \hline \end{array}$
5. $\begin{array}{r} 5 \\ -2 \\ \hline \end{array}$

6. $\begin{array}{r} 7 \\ -3 \\ \hline \end{array}$
7. $\begin{array}{r} 9 \\ -6 \\ \hline \end{array}$
8. $\begin{array}{r} 6 \\ -5 \\ \hline \end{array}$
9. $\begin{array}{r} 8 \\ -7 \\ \hline \end{array}$
10. $\begin{array}{r} 5 \\ -3 \\ \hline \end{array}$

Draw 4 things that come in sets of 2.

11.
2

12.
2

13.
2

14.
2

DAY 6

Subtract.

1. $10 - 5 =$ _____

2. $12 - 4 =$ _____

3. $14 - 4 =$ _____

4. $13 - 4 =$ _____

5. $15 - 5 =$ _____

6. $15 - 7 =$ _____

Make a pattern.
Draw ○ **in the** ◢, ⋛ **in the** ◁, **and** ⬭ **in the** ◯.

7.

DAY 7

Add.

1. $12 + 2 =$ _____   2. $13 + 3 =$ _____

3. $14 + 3 =$ _____   4. $15 + 4 =$ _____

5. $16 + 1 =$ _____   6. $19 + 1 =$ _____

7. Circle the odd answers.

8. Draw a rectangle around the even answers.

Add 10 minutes to each clock. Write the time.

9.

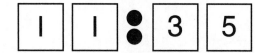

10.

11.

12.

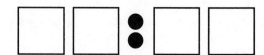

DAY 8

Make 100 tally marks.

1. ||||| |||||

2. Circle sets of 10.

3. How many sets of 10 equal 100? _____ sets

4. How many more sets of 10 to make 120? _____

Write the number.

5.

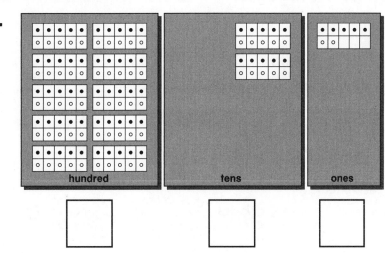

hundred   tens   ones

DAY 9

Add or subtract.

1. 6   2. 12   3. 5   4. 15   5. 13   6. 6
   +3   − 6   +8   − 9   − 4   +8
   ___   ___   ___   ___   ___   ___

Solve. Write the number sentence.

7. Joshua had 3 nickels.
   Jacob had 10 pennies.
   How much more money did
   Joshua have than Jacob?   ___¢ − ___¢ = ___¢

8. 6 goldfish and 8 snails
   live in an aquarium. How
   many are there all together?   ___ + ___ = ___

9. How many more snails
   are there than goldfish?   ___ − ___ = ___

10. If each fish cost 2¢,
    how much would
    3 fish cost?   ___¢ + ___¢ + ___¢ = ___¢

DAY 10 CHECKPOINT

Add.

1. $11 + 2 =$ _____
2. $6 + 7 =$ _____
3. $8 + 5 =$ _____

Subtract.

4. $10 - 5 =$ _____
5. $6 - 4 =$ _____
6. $4 - 0 =$ _____

Put an X on the coins that can be traded for a quarter.

7.    $=$

Solve.

8. Cory wants to buy 3 fish that cost 3¢ each.
   How much money does he need?

   ___¢ + ___¢ + ___¢ = ___¢

9. $126 =$ _____ _____ _____
   hundred   tens   ones

Finish the number pattern.

10. 2, 4, 6, _____, _____, _____, _____, _____, _____

DAY 11

Subtract.

1. $15 - 0 = $ _____

2. $15 - 2 = $ _____

3. $15 - 4 = $ _____

4. $15 - 6 = $ _____

5. $15 - 8 = $ _____

6. $15 - 10 = $ _____

7. $15 - 12 = $ _____

8. $15 - 14 = $ _____

9. Circle all the even answers.

10. Draw a triangle around the odd answers.

11. How many answers were even? _____

12. How many answers were odd? _____

Finish the number pattern.

13.   1,   3,   5,   7,   _____, _____, _____,

_____, _____, _____, _____, _____, _____, _____,

_____, _____, _____, _____, _____, _____, _____

DAY 12

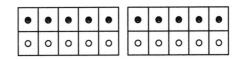

Subtract.

1. $15 - 0 = $ _____   2. $15 - 1 = $ _____

3. $15 - 3 = $ _____   4. $15 - 5 = $ _____

5. $15 - 7 = $ _____   6. $15 - 9 = $ _____

7. $15 - 11 = $ _____   8. $15 - 13 = $ _____

9. Circle all the even answers.

10. Draw a triangle around the odd answers.

11. How many answers were even? _____

12. How many answers were odd? _____

Put an X on the fewest coins.

DAY 13

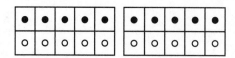

Subtract.

1. $15 - 3 = $ _____

2. $15 - 6 = $ _____

3. $15 - 7 = $ _____

4. $15 - 10 = $ _____

5. $15 - 5 = $ _____

6. $15 - 8 = $ _____

7. $15 - 13 = $ _____

8. $15 - 4 = $ _____

9. $15 - 1 = $ _____

10. Circle the even answers.

11. Draw a triangle around the odd answers.

Draw a picture using 2 half circles and 2 whole circles.
Add other shapes to complete.

12.

13. How many other shapes did you use?

DAY 14

Add.

1.   0
   3
+ 1
_____

2.   3
   4
+ 1
_____

3.   8
   3
+ 1
_____

4.   8
   7
+ 1
_____

5.   2
   1
+ 1
_____

6.   2
   5
+ 1
_____

7.   6
   5
+ 1
_____

8.   9
   6
+ 1
_____

Write the time to answer the questions.

9. What time is it? _____

10. Mary has to feed her cat in 15 minutes. What time will it be then? _____

11. 30 minutes ago, Brandon had an apple for a snack. What time did he eat the apple? _____

12. One hour from now, it will be time to make muffins. What time will we make muffins? _____

DAY 15

Add.

1. 1
   +4
   ___

2. 5
   +4
   ___

3. 9
   +4
   ___

4. 13
   + 4
   ___

5. 2
   +4
   ___

6. 6
   +4
   ___

7. 8
   +4
   ___

8. 12
   + 4
   ___

9. 16
   + 4
   ___

10. 3
   +4
   ___

11. 4
   +4
   ___

12. 7
   +4
   ___

13. Underline answers greater than 12.

14. Circle answers that are less than 12.

15. Put a check by the answers that are equal to 12.

Draw 4 things that come in 4's.

16.
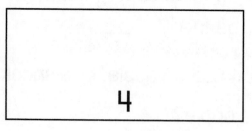
4

17.
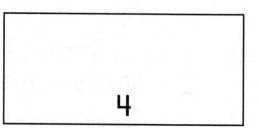
4

18.
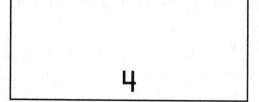
4

19.
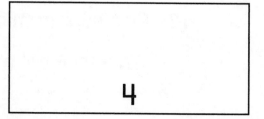
4

DAY 16

Add.

1.

$$10¢ \ + \ 5¢ \ + \ 2¢ = 17¢$$

2.

____¢ + ____¢ + ____¢ = ____¢

3.

____¢ + ____¢ + ____¢ = ____¢

4.

____¢ + ____¢ + ____¢ = ____¢

Make an A B B C pattern by drawing coins.

5. _____ _____ _____ _____ _____

_____ _____ _____ _____

DAY 17

Write the missing numbers.

1. _____ 80 _____ 82 _____ 84

2. _____ 101 _____ 103 _____ 105

3. _____ 122 _____ 124 _____ 126

4. _____ 143 _____ 145 _____ 147

5. Circle the numbers that have a 3 in the ones place.
   Color the circles yellow.

6. Circle the numbers that are even numbers.
   Color the circles orange.

7. What numbers are not circled? _____

Look at the shape.

8. Draw a smaller rectangle to the left of the square.
9. Draw a larger rectangle to the right of the square.
10. Draw a vertical line down the middle of the square.

DAY 18

Add or subtract.

1. $12 - 8 =$ _____

2. $6 + 7 =$ _____

3. $15 - 7 =$ _____

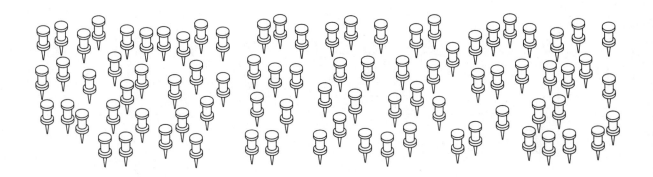

4. How many pins do you think there are? _____

5. Circle sets of 10.

   How many sets? _____   How many extras? _____

   | tens | ones |

6. How many in all?   _____   _____

Find the number of pins.

7. 6 sets and all the extras   _____   _____

8. 3 sets and no extras   _____   _____

9. 0 sets and the extras   _____   _____

10. 1 set and no extras   _____   _____

DAY 19

Add.

1. 4
   +9

2. 9
   +4

3. 4
   +7

4. 7
   +4

5. 4
   +4

6. 7
   +1

7. 8
   +4

8. 4
   +8

9. 15
   + 1

10. 17
    + 3

Solve. Write the number sentence.

11. Tim and Erin both have 6 rocks. How many rocks do they have all together?   ___ + ___ = ___

12. Gloria has 2 brothers. David has 3 brothers and 1 sister. How many more brothers does David have than Gloria?   ___ − ___ = ___

13. A frog has 4 legs and no tail. A tadpole has no legs and a long tail. How many more legs does the frog have than the tadpole?   ___ − ___ = ___

Subtract.

1. $\begin{array}{r} 14 \\ -10 \\ \hline \end{array}$ 2. $\begin{array}{r} 12 \\ -10 \\ \hline \end{array}$ 3. $\begin{array}{r} 10 \\ -5 \\ \hline \end{array}$ 4. $\begin{array}{r} 8 \\ -3 \\ \hline \end{array}$ 5. $\begin{array}{r} 6 \\ -1 \\ \hline \end{array}$

6. $\begin{array}{r} 13 \\ -5 \\ \hline \end{array}$ 7. $\begin{array}{r} 7 \\ -3 \\ \hline \end{array}$ 8. $\begin{array}{r} 11 \\ -6 \\ \hline \end{array}$ 9. $\begin{array}{r} 9 \\ -3 \\ \hline \end{array}$ 10. $\begin{array}{r} 5 \\ -3 \\ \hline \end{array}$

Solve.

11. 8 bones are in a dog dish. There are 2 dogs.
    Each dog gets the same number of bones.
    How many bones does each dog get? _____ bones
    Draw a picture.

MONTHLY ASSESSMENT

Look at the Calendar. Answer the questions.

1. If Monday, March 15, has a triangle on it, when will the next 4 triangles appear? _____

2. Color all the dates with a triangle orange.

3. If Friday, March 12, has a star on it, when will the next 4 stars appear? _____

4. Color all the dates with a star yellow.

5. If today is March 23, what will it be 7 days from now? Write the day, month, date, and year.

_____

MONTHLY ASSESSMENT

Add.

1. $11 + 2 =$ _____   2. $16 + 3 =$ _____

3. $12 + 2 =$ _____   4. $8 + 3 + 1 =$ _____

5. $12 + 2 + 1 =$ _____

Subtract.

6. $9 - 3 =$ _____   7. $14 - 4 =$ _____

8. $15 - 6 =$ _____   9. $15 - 4 =$ _____

10. $11 - 6 =$ _____

11. Circle all the odd answers.

Write the numbers in order.

12. 113, 110, 112, 109, 114, 111

_____

Write the number for 1 hundred, 6 tens, and 7 ones.

13. _____

Solve.

14. Steve has 2 nickels. Melissa has 16 pennies.
    How much more money does Melissa have than Steve? _____ ¢

MONTHLY ASSESSMENT

Add.

1.
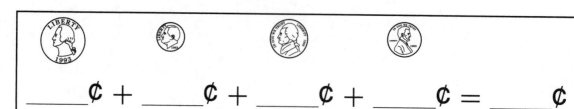

_____ ¢ + _____ ¢ + _____ ¢ + _____ ¢ = _____ ¢

2.
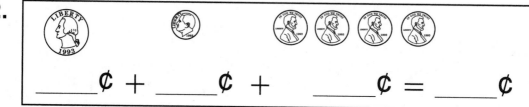

_____ ¢ + _____ ¢ + _____ ¢ = _____ ¢

Write the times.

3. What time is it? _____

4. What time will it be in 10 minutes? _____

5. What time was it 15 minutes ago? _____

Draw a line down the middle of each shape.
Draw a picture using the half shapes.

6.

DAY 1 · APRIL

Answer the questions.

1. Which months have 2 more birthdays than April?

   _____

2. Which month has 4 more birthdays than January?

   _____

3. Which 2 months together have 9 birthdays ?

   _____

4. Find 3 combinations of 7.

   _____

   _____

   _____

Label the pattern.

5.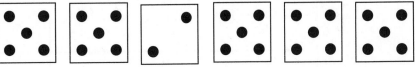

   A ___ ___ ___ ___ ___ ___ ___

DAY 2

Write the missing numbers.

1. $5 + \underline{\hspace{1cm}} = 10$
2. $3 + \underline{\hspace{1cm}} = 8$
3. $2 + \underline{\hspace{1cm}} = 9$
4. $10 - \underline{\hspace{1cm}} = 5$
5. $8 - \underline{\hspace{1cm}} = 5$
6. $9 - \underline{\hspace{1cm}} = 7$
7. $4 + \underline{\hspace{1cm}} = 9$
8. $9 - \underline{\hspace{1cm}} = 5$
9. $3 + \underline{\hspace{1cm}} = 6$
10. $4 + \underline{\hspace{1cm}} = 8$

Draw the coins. Use the letter to show which coin.

Q =   D =   N =   P =

	Number of coins	Amount	Coins to use
11.	3	30¢	
12.	3	31¢	
13.	3	20¢	
14.	3	45¢	

DAY 3

Write the missing numbers.

1. $2 + \underline{\hspace{1cm}} = 10$ 2. $4 + \underline{\hspace{1cm}} = 10$

3. $6 + \underline{\hspace{1cm}} = 10$ 4. $10 - \underline{\hspace{1cm}} = 8$

5. $10 - \underline{\hspace{1cm}} = 6$ 6. $10 - \underline{\hspace{1cm}} = 4$

7. $3 + \underline{\hspace{1cm}} = 8$ 8. $4 + \underline{\hspace{1cm}} = 8$

9. $7 + \underline{\hspace{1cm}} = 9$ 10. $10 - \underline{\hspace{1cm}} = 3$

Count each shape. Add.

11.

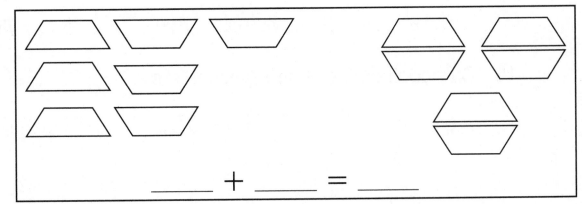

12.

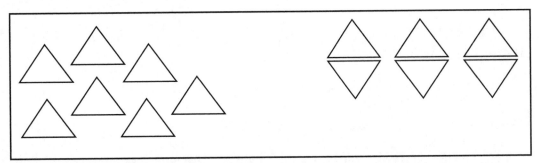

13.

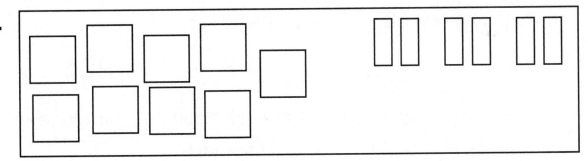

$\underline{\hspace{1.5cm}} + \underline{\hspace{1.5cm}} = \underline{\hspace{1.5cm}}$

DAY 4

Write the missing numbers.

1. $2 + \underline{\hspace{1cm}} = 7$

2. $4 + \underline{\hspace{1cm}} = 7$

3. $6 + \underline{\hspace{1cm}} = 7$

4. $7 + \underline{\hspace{1cm}} = 10$

5. $1 + \underline{\hspace{1cm}} = 10$

6. $5 + \underline{\hspace{1cm}} = 9$

7. $7 - \underline{\hspace{1cm}} = 5$

8. $10 - \underline{\hspace{1cm}} = 9$

9. $7 - \underline{\hspace{1cm}} = 1$

10. $7 - \underline{\hspace{1cm}} = 4$

11. $10 - \underline{\hspace{1cm}} = 3$

12. $9 - \underline{\hspace{1cm}} = 4$

Solve.

13. Luis had 4 coins in his bank. When he counted his money, he had 22¢. What did he have?

$\underline{\hspace{0.5cm}}¢ + \underline{\hspace{0.5cm}}¢ + \underline{\hspace{0.5cm}}¢ + \underline{\hspace{0.5cm}}¢ = 22¢$

14. Alyse had 6 coins. When she counted her money, she had 37¢. What did she have?

$\underline{\hspace{0.5cm}}¢ + \underline{\hspace{0.5cm}}¢ + \underline{\hspace{0.5cm}}¢ + \underline{\hspace{0.5cm}}¢ + \underline{\hspace{0.5cm}}¢ + \underline{\hspace{0.5cm}}¢ = 37¢$

15. Brandon has 3 coins that equal 31¢.

$\underline{\hspace{0.5cm}}¢ + \underline{\hspace{0.5cm}}¢ + \underline{\hspace{0.5cm}}¢ = 31¢$

DAY 5

Add.

1.	2.	3.	4.	5.
4	9	2	7	5
4	2	8	2	6
+ 4	+ 1	+ 2	+ 3	+ 2

6. $2 + 2 + 2 + 2 + 2 + 2 + 2 =$ _____

Solve. Show your work.

7.
There are 2 nickels in a dime.
How many nickels are
in 4 dimes?

_____

8.
There are 5 nickels in a quarter.
How many nickels are
in 2 quarters?

_____

DAY 6

Add dots. Make combinations of 6.

1. ☐ ☐ + = 6   2. ☐ ☐ + = 6

3. ☐ ☐ + = 6   4. ☐ ☐ + = 6

5. ☐ ☐ + = 6   6. ☐ ☐ + = 6

Continue the patterns.

7. b b p d b b p d b b

_ _ _ _ _ _ _ _

8. ○ ○ ☐ ○ ○ ☐ ___ ___ ___ ___

9. 9 9 6 3 9 9 6 3 ___ ___ ___ ___

DAY 7

Subtract.

1. $12 - \underline{} = 8$ 2. $14 - \underline{} = 7$

3. $15 - \underline{} = 9$ 4. $17 - \underline{} = 12$

5. $18 - \underline{} = 12$ 6. $19 - 5 = \underline{}$

7. $14 - \underline{} = 8$ 8. $20 - 7 = \underline{}$

9. $15 - \underline{} = 15$ 10. $13 - 8 = \underline{}$

Measure. Use the ruler.

11. Color 6 inches blue.

12. Color 6 inches of pennies brown.

13. Draw something that is 6 inches long.

DAY 8

Subtract.

1. 18 − 6	2. 8 − 6	3. 16 − 4	4. 6 − 4	5. 20 − 15	6. 10 −5

7. 19 − 3	8. 17 − 3	9. 13 − 3	10. 9 − 3	11. 7 − 3	12. 12 − 3

Write the number.

13.
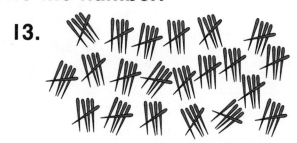

14.

15.
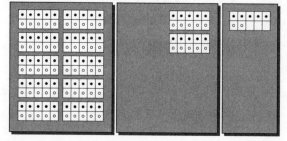

hundred	tens	ones	= number

DAY 9

Add.

1. $6 + 8 + 2 =$ ____   2. $9 + 4 + 2 =$ ____

3. $17 + 1 + 2 =$ ____   4. $12 + 6 + 2 =$ ____

5. $11 + 5 + 2 =$ ____   6. $15 + 3 + 2 =$ ____

Solve. Show your work.

Circle yes or no.

7. Nalah has 17¢. She wants to buy a puzzle that costs 50¢. Her brother gives her 22¢. Does she have enough money?	$+$ _____ yes no
8. Antonio has 42¢. He got 2 quarters for his birthday. He wants to buy a dinosaur that cost 75¢. Can he buy it?	$+$ _____ $-$ _____ yes no
9. Alex has 2 quarters and a dime. He wants to get 2 bananas for lunch. Each banana cost 10¢. Can he buy 2 bananas?	$+$ _____ $-$ _____ yes no

Write the missing numbers.

1. 12 − _____ = 6
2. 14 − _____ = 6
3. 17 − _____ = 12
4. 14 + _____ = 20
5. 13 + _____ = 18
6. 3 + _____ = 17

Draw an X on the coins.

7. 4 coins   37 ¢

8. 6 coins   51¢

Make a shape. Use the 2 shapes in the box.

9.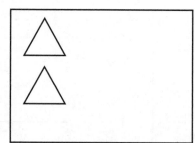

10.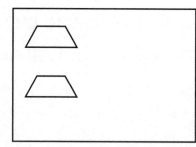

11.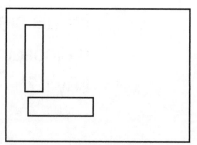

Make an ABCC pattern.

12. _____ _____ _____ _____ _____ _____ _____ _____
    A   B   C   C   A   B   C   C

DAY 11

Add.

1. 🧤🧤 + 🧤🧤 + 🧤🧤 + 🧤🧤 + 🧤🧤 + 🧤🧤 = ____

2. 🚲 + 🚲 + 🚲 + 🚲 + 🚲 + 🚲 = ____

3. ⊡⊡ + ⊡⊡ + ⊡⊡ + ⊡⊡ + ⊡⊡ = ____

4. $2 + 2 + 2 + 2 + 2 + 2 + 2 + 2 =$ ____

Complete the pattern.

5. ● ☐ ☐ ● ☐ ● ☐ ☐ ● ☐ __ __ __ __

    A   B   B   A   B   A   B   B   A   B   A   B   B   A   B

6. + − − + − __ __ __ __ __ __ __ __ __

    A   B   B   A   B   A   B   B   A   B   A   B   B   A   B

Label the pattern.

7. ● ☐ ☐ ● ☐ ● ☐ ☐ ● ☐ ● ☐ ☐ ● ☐

    __ __ __ __ __ __ __ __ __ __ __ __ __ __ __

Is the sum 10? Circle the answer.

1. yes   no

2. yes   no

3. yes   no

4. yes   no

5. yes   no

6. yes   no

7. yes   no

8. yes   no

9. yes   no

Measure. Use the ruler.

| 1 | 2 | 3 | 4 | 5 | 6 |

10. 1 2 3 4 5 6   _____ inches

11. 1 2 3 4 5 6 7 8 9 10 11 12   _____ inches

12. 1 2 3 4 5 6 7 8 9 10 11 12 13 14 15 16 17 18   _____ inches

DAY 13

Use the numbers in the grid.

91	92	93	94	95	96	97	98	99	100
101	102	103	104	105	106	107	108	109	110
111	112	113	114	115	116	117	118	119	120
121	122	123	124	125	126	127	128	129	130

Add 5.

1. 104 _____　　2. 96 _____　　3. 108 _____

Subtract 4.

4. 111 _____　　5. 86 _____　　6. 130 _____

Make new shapes.

7. Draw a line from the corner with the star to the corner with the dot.

8. Do the same to the other 3 corners.

9. Color the top shape yellow.

10. Color the right shape red.

11. Color the bottom shape blue.

12. Color the left shape green.

13. How many shapes did you make?

_____ trapezoids

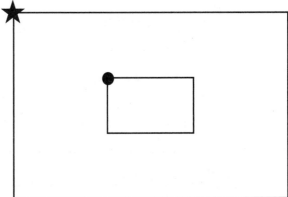

DAY 14

Draw an X under the dominoes that make the sum of 8.
Find 6 ways.

		·	··	··	··	··	··	··	··	··
1.	8								X	
2.	8									
3.	8									
4.	8									
5.	8									
6.	8									

Solve. Write the number sentence.

7. Justin knew that 7 + 2 = 9.
    He wanted to add 7 more.
    Find the sum.

    _____   _____   _____

8. Rosie knew that 5 + 4 = 9. She
    added 10 more. Find the sum.

    _____   _____   _____

9. Laurie knew that Justin and Rosie
    found the sums. Laurie wanted to
    know the difference between
    Justin's and Rosie's answers.

    _____ — _____ = _____

DAY 15

Subtract.

1. $15 - 4 = $ _____

2. $12 - 4 = $ _____

3. $8 - 4 = $ _____

4. $10 - 4 = $ _____

5. $13 - 4 = $ _____

6. $7 - 4 = $ _____

7. $14 - 4 = $ _____

8. $11 - 4 = $ _____

9. $6 - 4 = $ _____

10. $5 - 4 = $ _____

11. $9 - 4 = $ _____

12. $4 - 4 = $ _____

Solve.

13. Bicycles have 2 wheels. How many wheels are on 5 bikes? Show your work.

_____ wheels on _____ bikes

14. Dogs have 4 legs and 1 tail. How many legs and how many tails do 4 dogs have?

_____ legs and _____ tails

Add.

1. $16 + 2 = \underline{\hspace{1cm}}$ 2. $20 + 2 = \underline{\hspace{1cm}}$

3. $13 + 2 = \underline{\hspace{1cm}}$ 4. $17 + 2 = \underline{\hspace{1cm}}$

5. $18 + 2 = \underline{\hspace{1cm}}$ 6. $8 + 2 = \underline{\hspace{1cm}}$

7. $12 + 2 = \underline{\hspace{1cm}}$ 8. $9 + 2 = \underline{\hspace{1cm}}$

9. $10 + 2 = \underline{\hspace{1cm}}$ 10. $6 + 2 = \underline{\hspace{1cm}}$

11. $15 + 2 = \underline{\hspace{1cm}}$ 12. $4 + 2 = \underline{\hspace{1cm}}$

13. $14 + 2 = \underline{\hspace{1cm}}$ 14. $2 + 2 = \underline{\hspace{1cm}}$

15. $11 + 2 = \underline{\hspace{1cm}}$ 16. $8 + 4 = \underline{\hspace{1cm}}$

Choose 2 colors. Color the pattern.

17.

A	B	B	A	B	A	B	B	A	B	A	B	B	A	B

Write the missing numbers.

18. 1 2 2 1 2 1 __ __ 1 __ 1 __ __

1 __ 1 2 2 __ 2 __ __ __ __

DAY 17

Add.

1.

$$25¢ + 10¢ + 10¢ + 1¢ = \underline{\qquad}¢$$

2.

$$25¢ + 25¢ + 5¢ = \underline{\qquad}¢$$

3.

$$25¢ + 10¢ + 10¢ + 10¢ + 5¢ = \underline{\qquad}¢$$

Find 3 ways to make 30¢. Use the letters for the coins.

(Q) = quarter   (D) = dime   (N) = nickel   (P) = penny

4.

$$= 30¢$$

5.

$$= 30¢$$

6.

$$= 30¢$$

DAY 18

Subtract.

1. $16 - 2 = $ _____

2. $11 - 2 = $ _____

3. $13 - 2 = $ _____

4. $10 - 2 = $ _____

5. $18 - 2 = $ _____

6. $4 - 2 = $ _____

7. $12 - 2 = $ _____

8. $2 - 2 = $ _____

9. $17 - 2 = $ _____

10. $8 - 2 = $ _____

11. $15 - 2 = $ _____

12. $6 - 2 = $ _____

13. $14 - 2 = $ _____

14. $9 - 2 = $ _____

15. $20 - 2 = $ _____

16. $7 - 5 = $ _____

17. Put a check mark by the odd answers.

18. Circle the answers less than 5.

Write the number.

19. 1 hundred , 5 tens, and 8 ones = _____

20. 9 tens and 9 ones   = _____

21. 2 hundreds, 4 tens, and 0 ones = _____

22. 7 tens and 1 one   = _____

DAY 19

Write the missing numbers.

	1.	2.	3.	4.	5.
	18	6	12	8	18
−					
	14	4	7	7	6

	6.	7.	8.	9.	10.
	15	5	19	7	17
+					
	19	18	21	20	20

11. Circle the even answers.

12. Put a check mark next to answers greater than 12.

Solve. Write the number sentence.

13. 12 birds were in a tree. A cat ran
up the tree and 8 birds flew away.
How many birds are in the tree?   ____ ____ = ____

14. The puppy is white with
14 brown spots. The cat is
brown with 7 black spots.
How many more spots does
the dog have?   ____ ____ = ____

15. Sergio ate 2 apples, 1 orange,
and 3 crackers. How much fruit
did he eat?   ____ ____ = ____

Place an X under the dominoes to make the sum of 10. Find 8 ways.

	1	2	3	4	5	6	7	8	9
1. 10		X	X		X				
2. 10									
3. 10									
4. 10									
5. 10									
6. 10									
7. 10									
8. 10									

Write number sentences to show the 8 ways to make 10.

1. $2 + 3 + 5 = 10$ 2. _____

3. _____   4. _____

5. _____   6. _____

7. _____   8. _____

MONTHLY ASSESSMENT

Look at the Calendar. Answer the questions.

1. Color the dates with squares around them yellow.
   Write the numbers.

   _____

2. What 2 ways are these numbers alike?

   _____

3. Color the dates with triangles around them orange. What
   pattern do the triangle numbers follow?

   _____

MONTHLY ASSESSMENT

Add.

1. $16 + 4 =$ _____

2. $15 + 3 =$ _____

3. $3 + 12 =$ _____

4. $5 + 13 =$ _____

Subtract.

5. $14 - 5 =$ _____

6. $12 - 6 =$ _____

7. $19 - 11 =$ _____

8. $15 - 7 =$ _____

Write the missing numbers.

9. $14 +$ _____ $= 20$

10. $5 +$ _____ $=$ _____

11. $17 -$ _____ $=$ _____

12. $16 - 7 =$ _____

Solve.

13. Ashley has 12 cookies to share with 3 friends. She wants to make sure that she and her friends each get the same number of cookies. How many cookies will each child get?

_____ cookies

Draw a picture to show your answer.

MONTHLY ASSESSMENT

Draw as many diamonds as you can. Use 8 triangles.

1.

Draw a picture using 6 trapezoids.

2.

Show the coins that can make 50¢. Use letters.

Q = quarter   D = dime   N = nickel   P = penny

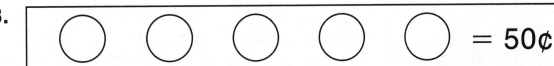

3.

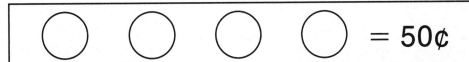

4.

5.

6. Can you make 50¢ with 3 coins?   yes   no

Measure. Use a ruler.

7. Color enough squares to equal 5 inches.

Make 2 numbers. Circle the number that is greater.

1. 1 and 6 = 16 (61)

2. 7 and 5 =

3. 2 and 4 =

4. 9 and 4 =

5. 3 and 1 =

6. 4 and 8 =

7. 4 and 0 =

8. 9 and 7 =

9. Color each circle that has an answer that is even and is less than 50.

What is a pattern?

10. Is this a pattern? yes no

    A

11. Explain your answer.

    _____

12. Name 5 patterns that could begin like this.

    _____

    _____

DAY 2

Complete the fact families.

1.
$$
\begin{array}{r} 8 \\ + 2 \\ \hline \end{array}
$$

2.
$$
\begin{array}{r} 2 \\ + 8 \\ \hline \end{array}
$$

3.
$$
\begin{array}{r} 10 \\ - 2 \\ \hline \end{array}
$$

4.
$$
\begin{array}{r} 10 \\ - 8 \\ \hline \end{array}
$$

5.
$$
\begin{array}{r} 6 \\ + 4 \\ \hline \end{array}
$$

6.
$$
\begin{array}{r} 4 \\ + 6 \\ \hline \end{array}
$$

7.
$$
\begin{array}{r} 10 \\ - 4 \\ \hline \end{array}
$$

8.
$$
\begin{array}{r} 10 \\ - 6 \\ \hline \end{array}
$$

What is a pattern?

9.   Is this a pattern?   yes   no

10. Name 4 patterns that could begin like this.

_____

_____

Make change for a quarter.

		Cost	Change		
11.	⚾	15¢	___	___	___
12.	▱	10¢	___	___	___
13.	♡	12¢	___	___	___
14.	🍦	22¢	___	___	___

DAY 3

Complete the fact families.

1.
$$7 + 3$$

2.
$$3 + 7$$

3.
$$10 - 7$$

4.
$$10 - 3$$

5.
$$9 + 1$$

6.
$$1 + 9$$

7.
$$10 - 9$$

8.
$$10 - 1$$

What is a pattern?

9.   Is this a pattern?   yes   no

10. Name 4 patterns that could begin like this.

_____

_____

Complete the matching half of the shape.

11.

12.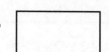

13.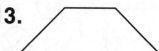

14.

15.

16.

DAY 4

Write the missing numbers.

1. $12 - \underline{} = 4$ 2. $6 + \underline{} = 13$

3. $3 + 14 = \underline{}$ 4. $9 + 9 = \underline{}$

5. $\underline{} - 7 = 7$ 6. $2 + \underline{} = 13$

What is a pattern?

7. 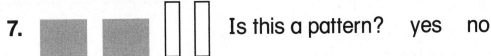 Is this a pattern?   yes   no

8. Name 3 patterns that could begin like this.

_____

Solve.

9. Jordan had 6 smooth brown rocks. He gave 3 of his rocks to Elaine. How many rocks does Jordan have?

   _____ − _____ = _____ rocks

   Does he have more than, less than, or the same number of rocks as Elaine? Circle the answer.

   more than   less than   same

10. Elaine found 4 more smooth rocks at the river. How many rocks does Elaine have now?

   _____ + _____ = _____ rocks

   Does she have more than, less than, or the same number of rocks as Jordan? Circle the answer.

   more than   less than   same

DAY 5

Write the missing numbers.

1. (107) (109) ( ) (113) ( ) ( )

2. (44) (46) ( ) (50) ( ) ( )

What is a pattern?

3. ▨ ▨ ▯ ▯ ▭   Is this a pattern?   yes   no

4. Name 2 patterns that could begin like this.

_____

Solve.

5. A tricycle has 3 tires.

How many tires do 6 tricycles have? _____ tires

Draw a picture to show your answer.

DAY 6

Make 2 numbers. Circle the number that is less.

1. 4 and 9 = (49) 94
2. 4 and 5 =

3. 3 and 5 =
4. 9 and 8 =

5. 7 and 6 =
6. 5 and 1 =

7. 9 and 2 =
8. 6 and 4 =

9. Color each circle that has an answer that is odd and is greater than 50.

What is a pattern?

10. Is this a pattern?   yes   no

11. Explain your answer.

_____

_____

12. Why have your predictions changed during the week?

_____

13. Draw a pattern that could begin like this.

DAY 7

Write the missing numbers.

1. 4
   + 5
   ‾‾‾

2.   5
   + ☐
   ‾‾‾
     9

3.   9
   − 4
   ‾‾‾

4.   9
   − ☐
   ‾‾‾
     4

5.   2
   + 6
   ‾‾‾

6.   6
   + ☐
   ‾‾‾
     8

7.   8
   − ☐
   ‾‾‾
     6

8.   8
   − ☐
   ‾‾‾
     2

What is a pattern?

9.

   Is this a pattern?   yes   no

Circle the answer to complete the sentence.

10.   holds   more   less   than   .

11.    holds   more   less   than   .

12.   holds   more   less   than    .

13.    holds   more   less   than   .

DAY 8

Add.

1. 10¢
   + 20¢

2. 40¢
   + 30¢

3. 60¢
   + 10¢

4. 30¢
   + 10¢

5. 20¢
   + 60¢

6. 70¢
   + 20¢

7. 50¢
   + 30¢

8. 80¢
   + 10¢

What is a pattern?

9.

Is this a pattern?   yes   no

Write the numbers.

71							

10. 8 tens 4 ones

11. 7 tens 2 ones

12. 8 tens 8 ones

13. all the numbers with 9 tens

14. 7 tens 9 ones

15. 7 tens 6 ones

DAY 9

Subtract.

1.
$$60¢$$
$$-40¢$$

2.
$$40¢$$
$$-30¢$$

3.
$$30¢$$
$$-20¢$$

4.
$$20¢$$
$$-10¢$$

5.
$$70¢$$
$$-50¢$$

6.
$$50¢$$
$$-30¢$$

7.
$$80¢$$
$$-40¢$$

8.
$$90¢$$
$$-40¢$$

What is a pattern?

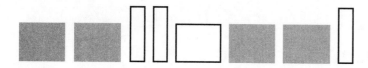

9. How many more shapes are needed to form a pattern? _____

Solve. Write the number sentence.

10. Jan has read 7 books about snakes. Lucas has read 3 books about turtles. Nick has read 4 books about dinosaurs. How many books have they read all together?

_____ + _____ + _____ = _____

11. Mom bought 4 cans of cherries. We made a pie with 2 cans. How many cans of cherries are left?

_____ − _____ = _____

DAY 10   CHECKPOINT

Circle the numbers greater than 60.
Draw a box around the odd numbers.

1. 16   61   48   84   97   79   108

What is a pattern?

2.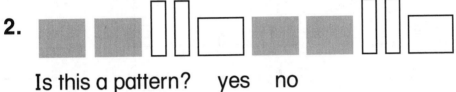

Is this a pattern?   yes   no

3. Explain your answer.

_____

Solve.

4. Sam had 25¢. He spent 15¢. How much change did Sam get back?

25¢ − _____¢ = _____¢

Circle the answer.

5. more than   less than   the same

6. more than   less than   the same

7. more than   less than   the same   3 + 4

8. 25¢   more than   less than   the same

Write 8 number sentences for 10.

1. _____ + _____ = 10   2. _____ − _____ = 10

3. _____ + _____ = 10   4. _____ − _____ = 10

5. _____ + _____ = 10   6. _____ − _____ = 10

7. _____ + _____ = 10   8. _____ − _____ = 10

Label the pattern.

9.
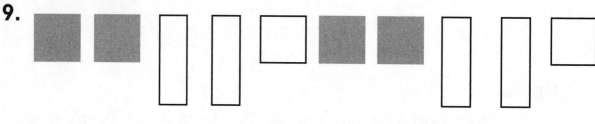

_____ _____ _____ _____ _____ _____ _____ _____ _____ _____ _____

Make the same pattern with different pictures.
Label the pattern.

10.

<u>A</u> __ __ __ __ __ __ __ __ __ __

Write the missing numbers.

11. 1, 1, 2, 2, 3, 1, _____, _____, _____, 3, _____, 1

DAY 12

Write 8 number sentences for 8.

1. _____ + _____ = 8   2. _____ − _____ = 8

3. _____ + _____ = 8   4. _____ − _____ = 8

5. _____ + _____ = 8   6. _____ − _____ = 8

7. _____ + _____ = 8   8. _____ − _____ = 8

Color the number of cups.

9.   10.   11.

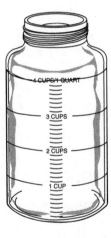

   2 cups   **3 cups**   **4 cups**

12. Draw a box around the jar that holds the most.

13. Put an X on the jar that holds the least.

DAY 13

Write the missing numbers.

1. $12 - \underline{\hphantom{00}} = 6$ 2. $14 - \underline{\hphantom{00}} = 8$

3. $16 - 6 = \underline{\hphantom{00}}$ 4. $18 - 10 = \underline{\hphantom{00}}$

5. $6 + \underline{\hphantom{00}} = 12$ 6. $8 + \underline{\hphantom{00}} = 14$

7. $6 + \underline{\hphantom{00}} = 16$ 8. $\underline{\hphantom{00}} + 10 = 18$

9. $10 - 10 = \underline{\hphantom{00}}$ 10. $8 + \underline{\hphantom{00}} = 16$

Sort the shapes.

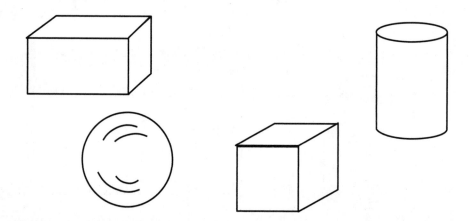

11. Color the shapes that can roll red.

12. Underline shapes that can be stacked.

13. Draw one of the shapes.

DAY 14

Solve.

Write the number sentence and draw the change.

Q = quarter   D = dime   N = nickel   P = penny

1. Manny has 25¢. He wants to buy a game of checkers to play with his friend Monica. How much change will Manny get?

   _____

2. Robert has 25¢. He wants to buy a tablet and one crayon so that he can draw. He also needs an eraser. How much change will he get?

   _____   _____

3. Miyo has 25¢. She buys the apple and the yo-yo. How much change does Miyo get?

   _____   _____

DAY 15

Write 8 number sentences for 9.

1. _____ + _____ = 9   2. _____ − _____ = 9

3. _____ + _____ = 9   4. _____ − _____ = 9

5. _____ + _____ = 9   6. _____ − _____ = 9

7. _____ + _____ = 9   8. _____ − _____ = 9

Write < or >.

9. 85 ◯ 56   10. 20 ◯ 31   11. 48 ◯ 88

Use dimes. Show 4 ways to make 90¢.

30¢ + 60¢ = 90¢

12. _____¢ + _____¢ = 90¢

13. _____¢ + _____¢ = 90¢

14. _____¢ + _____¢ = 90¢

15. _____¢ + _____¢ = 90¢

DAY 16

Add.

1. 10¢ + 5¢ + 5¢ + 1¢ + 1¢ = _____¢

2. 25¢ + 5¢ + 1¢ + 1¢ = _____¢

3. 25¢ + 25¢ + 1¢ + 1¢ + 1¢ = _____¢

4. 10¢ + 10¢ + 5¢ + 5¢ + 1¢ + 1¢ = _____¢

5. 25¢ + 10¢ + 10¢ + 1¢ + 1¢ + 1¢ = _____¢

6. Circle the number sentences that have the same answer.

Complete the number patterns.

7. 5, 10, 15, ____, ____, ____, ____, ____, ____

8. 1, 3, 5, ____, ____, ____, ____, ____, ____

9. 2, 4, 6, ____, ____, ____, ____, ____, ____

10. 1, 4, 7, 10, ____, ____, ____, ____, ____

11. 1, 1, 7, 1, 1, 7, ____, ____, ____, ____, ____

DAY 17

Subtract.

1. 25¢ − 15¢ = ____ ¢   2. 25¢ − 5¢ = ____ ¢

3. 10¢ − 3¢ = ____ ¢   4. 5¢ − 3¢ = ____ ¢

5. 15¢ − 10¢ = ____ ¢   6. 15¢ − 5¢ = ____ ¢

7. 10¢ − 5¢ = ____ ¢   8. 5¢ − 5¢ = ____ ¢

Measure.

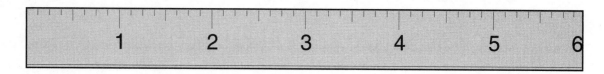

9. Draw a crayon that is 3 inches long.

10. Draw a pencil that is 6 inches long.

11. Draw a striped worm that is 4 inches long.

Add.

1. $8 + 3 =$ _____

2. $10 + 3 =$ _____

3. $12 + 3 =$ _____

4. $14 + 3 =$ _____

5. $16 + 3 =$ _____

6. $7 + 3 =$ _____

7. $9 + 3 =$ _____

8. $11 + 3 =$ _____

9. $13 + 3 =$ _____

10. $4 + 8 =$ _____

Write the numbers.

11. 1 hundred   3 tens   6 ones $=$ 136

12. 1 hundred   9 tens   4 ones $=$ _____

13. 1 hundred   3 tens   3 ones $=$ _____

14. 1 hundred   8 tens   9 ones $=$ _____

15. 1 hundred   6 tens   7 ones $=$ _____

16. 2 hundreds   3 tens   8 ones $=$ _____

17. 2 hundreds   4 tens   6 ones $=$ _____

DAY 19

Add 4 to each number.

1. 6 ···· __10__   2. 5 ···· __9__   3. 15 ···· __19__

4. 3 _____   5. 2 _____   6. 11 _____

7. 4 _____   8. 7 _____   9. 12 _____

10. 8 _____   11. 17 _____   12. 16 _____

Solve. Write the number sentences.

13. Zane has a few baseball cards. He needs 3 more cards to have 10 cards. How many cards does Zane have?

    _____ − _____ = _____

14. Julia had 10¢ in her piggy bank. Her mom gave her a nickel and her grandfather gave her 3¢. How much money does Julia have in her bank?

    _____¢ + _____¢ + _____¢ = _____¢

15. Antonio has 2 boxes of crayons with 8 crayons in each box. How many crayons does he have?

    _____ + _____ = _____

DAY 20

Subtract 4.

1. 6 •••• _2_ 2. 8 •••• _4_ 3. 10 •••• _6_

4. 4 ____ 5. 9 ____ 6. 12 ____

7. 5 ____ 8. 11 ____ 9. 10 ____

10. 7 ____ 11. 15 ____ 12. 13 ____

Write the missing numbers.

13. | ____ + ____ + ____ = 10 |

14. | ____ + ____ + ____ = 12 |

15. | ____ + ____ + ____ = 9 |

16. | ____ + ____ + ____ = 8 |

17. | ____ + ____ + ____ = 15 |

MONTHLY ASSESSMENT

Look at the Calendar.
Answer the questions.

1. Complete the B pattern on the Calendar.

2. Write in the number 29 and draw in the pattern shape. What day does 29 fall on?

_____

3. Count back 5 days and write the number. Draw the pattern shape. What is the day and date?

_____

4. What numbers make up the A pattern?

_____

5. Describe the A number pattern.

_____

MONTHLY ASSESSMENT

Write the missing numbers.

1.
$$\begin{array}{r} \boxed{} \\ +\ 6 \\ \hline 8 \end{array}$$

2.
$$\begin{array}{r} \boxed{} \\ +\ 2 \\ \hline 8 \end{array}$$

3.
$$\begin{array}{r} \boxed{} \\ +\ 6 \\ \hline 10 \end{array}$$

4.
$$\begin{array}{r} \boxed{} \\ +\ 4 \\ \hline 10 \end{array}$$

5.
$$\begin{array}{r} \boxed{} \\ +\ 5 \\ \hline 9 \end{array}$$

6.
$$\begin{array}{r} \boxed{} \\ +\ 6 \\ \hline 9 \end{array}$$

7.
$$\begin{array}{r} 12 \\ -\ \boxed{} \\ \hline 2 \end{array}$$

8.
$$\begin{array}{r} 10 \\ -\ \boxed{} \\ \hline 0 \end{array}$$

9.
$$\begin{array}{r} 16 \\ -\ \boxed{} \\ \hline 6 \end{array}$$

10.
$$\begin{array}{r} 14 \\ -\ \boxed{} \\ \hline 4 \end{array}$$

Solve. Write the number sentence.

11. Ryan kicked 3 soccer goals. Tyra kicked 4 goals. How many goals did they kick? _____

12. Ryan and Tyra's team won the game. Their team had 10 goals. How many goals were not kicked by Tyra or Ryan?

_____

13. Dennis has 10 small red balls. He wants to share with 4 of his friends. He wants to make sure that he and his friends have the same number of balls. Draw a picture to show how many balls each person should get.

MONTHLY ASSESSMENT

Draw the other half of the shape. Color the shapes that can be stacked red.

1. 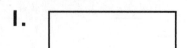   2.    3.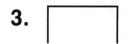

4.   5.   6.

Group the nickels 2 ways. Write the number sentences to show the ways.

7. ___ + ___ = ___   8. ___ + ___ = ___

Measure.

9. Color the first jar so that it holds more than the second jar.

10. Color the third jar so that it holds less than the first and second jar.

11. Color the fourth jar so that it holds the same as the second jar.